My Kids Don't Live With Me Anymore

COPING WITH THE CUSTODY CRISIS

DOREEN VIRTUE

CompCare®Publishers

2415 Annapolis Lane
Minneapolis, Minnesota 55441

Library of Congress Cataloging-in-Publication Data

Virtue, Doreen, 1958–
    My kids don't live with me anymore.

    Bibliography: p.
    Includes index.
    1. Divorce—United States.   2. Divorced parents—
United States.   3. Custody of children—United States.
I. Title.
HQ834.V57 1988   306.8'9'0973   88-25763

Cover design by Jeremy Gale

Inquiries, orders, and catalog requests should be addressed to
CompCare Publishers
2415 Annapolis Lane
Minneapolis, MN 55441
Call toll free 800/328-3330
(Minnesota residents 559-4800)

5   4   3   2   1
92   91   90   89   88

To my children,
Chuck and Grant,
with love

Contents

Acknowledgments

A lot of people helped in the creation and completion of this book, and I appreciate their support and encouragement so much. My husband, Dwight Virtue, was not only helpful but also extremely patient during all those long hours I spent holed up in my office typing away. He believed in this book all along, even during those times when my own faith was wavering. And far from being threatened by the amount of time I've put into this and other projects, Dwight has always been happy for us, always ready to support every endeavor I begin. Thanks for everything, sweetheart!

The folks at CompCare were incredibly helpful, as well, and I want to especially thank Bonnie Hesse, who is a uniquely talented individual with a wonderful background blending psychology and literature together. Thank you, too, to Margaret Marsh for believing in this project, Kathy Garrett for her insightful editing and friendship, Diane Davis for her enthusiastic assistance, Elaine Wogensen for her help during the book's infancy and early childhood, and Pat McCullough for providing much encouragement.

Thank you to my parents, Bill and Joan Hannan, for encouraging me to write all along (and Dad, thanks for the help with the editing!). A most grateful thank you to Jim Talley, a great man and a great attorney, who stuck with me through thick and thin during my second custody case. I also want to say thank you so much to Dr. Stephen Doyne who was so caring and thorough as he evaluated my custody case and was so instrumental in the events of my second custody case.

A warm thank you to my friends who stuck with me during the highs and lows of my custody crisis, and who really know the true meaning of friendship—Melinda White, Dan Matzke and Dianna Whitfield. I also want to thank Dr. Dee Sheperd-Look of California State University, Northridge, Dave Allec, Diane Hunt, Rickie Gherardi, and Tara Borek for their invaluable assistance during the writing of this book. Thank you, too, to Blair Kuropatkin for her help as I was coming out of the "custody closet."

To the wonderful women of Mothers Without Custody, a bouquet of thanks. Especially helpful were Angie Mease, Elaine Lane, Carolyn Sage-Hemingway and Cathy Knapp.

And finally, a heartfelt thank you to the men and women who share their stories in the pages of this book in order to help others.

Introduction
I Never Thought It Could Happen to Me

Some marriages die a slow, silent death. Not mine. No, my marriage became a loud and painful forum for two adults to viciously attack each other with words. Soon after our second child was born, my husband of three years and I began taking out on each other our frustrations over unrealized dreams and an intolerably tight budget. I blamed him for my personal unhappiness and he blamed me for his. Suddenly, it seemed to both of us that our marriage was a prison. There was no joy. No love. Only fighting and bitterness.

My husband's incessant put-downs and control over my daily itinerary, finances and transportation had left me feeling incompetent and worthless. Never before had I felt so utterly stupid, unattractive, or unwanted. We tried marriage counseling and a trial separation, but everything seemed to point to the obviously impending divorce. I became obsessed with getting myself and my two sons out of the tense and explosive atmosphere of our small apartment. The decision to divorce came quickly after our fourth year of marriage.

I packed up the children, Chuck and Grant, then 3 and 1½ years old, and drove to my parents' house not far from where we lived. But, as much as they wanted to help, my mother and father were not in a position to have us all move in permanently. My mother had some serious health problems coupled with career burnout. She was unable to withstand much activity or noise—two inevitables with young children around.

And I knew, deep down, as things stood I could not single-handedly raise my two young sons. A college student at the time, I had no money or job and nothing in sight which would enable me to support the three of us. The thought of the three of us on welfare, living in a crime-infested neighborhood, dressing in Salvation Army clothes and worrying about our next meal sickened me. It was immediately clear to my parents and me that Chuck and Grant would have to temporarily reside with their dad until I could get on my feet financially. But today I still believe it was the part of me that didn't like or believe in myself that ultimately led me to make the decision to allow my sons to go and live with their father.

That Thursday night in October was the most horrible night of my life. As I buckled my two crying sons into my father's car for the return trip to my soon-to-be ex-husband, I tried to reassure them—and myself—that they'd be going bye-bye for just a little while. I told them, "Mommy will come and get you just as soon as I can." As my father drove away, I was numbed by the gravity of the moment. I remember thinking, this nightmare is not happening to me. Please, please, let it be happening to someone else.

In the winter months that followed, I went through the motions of going to college each day, living with my parents, riding the bus to campus. The weeks blurred together. I reeled from confusion and disbelief.

But by the spring, my feelings seemed to thaw out, and I began to throw all my energy into getting my boys back with me again. I talked to my lawyer constantly about how we'd regain custody. Up until the day I walked into family law court almost fourteen months after buckling my boys into the car that night, I was thoroughly convinced that, as the mother, I would automatically be awarded primary physical custody.

As my lawyer held open the courtroom door for my mother and me, I asked him what he thought my chances were of getting custody of the children right away. He averted his eyes and fumbled as he breathed the words, "You're not getting custody." Two minutes later, we were seated in front of the judge. He ordered me to pay three hundred dollars per month in child support to my ex-husband, who was being awarded custody of my two babies. I listened in disbelief as the judge explained the process of "status quo": that the children would remain where they had been residing after the divorce, unless a problem could be proven to exist. He also cited the fact that my husband was, and would be in the future, better off financially. I thought, "No! No! You're making a big mistake!" and leaned forward to tell that to the judge, but my attorney put a firm hand on my shoulder and motioned for me not to make a scene.

I sat there, stinging like a burn victim. And I felt utterly, indescribably helpless. "This has got to be the Twilight Zone. The kids belong with me. *I'M THEIR MOTHER!*"

At that time, I had *never* heard of a woman losing custody unless she was legally unfit. During that first year after the custody decision, nothing and no one could make me feel better, and my self-esteem sank to new lows. I spent almost every evening in tears. During the day I continued my college work, earning my degree in psychology, alone with my loss.

Then, my life took a new turn when I went to work as a counselor at a local alcohol and drug abuse inpatient center. I found that many of my clients, male and female, had also lost custody of their children. They, too, stated that they felt alone in their grief, not really understanding the emotional devastation they had endured. And why, when they finally got to see their kids, were the visitations so traumatic? We worked on these issues together.

At a certain point I began to seek out other people through national support groups for noncustodial parents. I finally let go of more of my own pain in meeting and getting to know personally hundreds of parents struggling with the same problems I saw in my clients and had lived through myself. Also, I learned that many parents who *had* primary custody also suffered, grieved, were angry and afraid, when their children were away on visitations.

But what I couldn't find was any written material that would help these men and women feel better about themselves and their situations. There were no books to let mothers and fathers without custody know that they were not alone in their feelings. There was no self-help book that could have saved my own self-concept from hitting rock bottom following my custody loss. So, I decided to write the book I had desperately needed to read. A book full of accounts of other men and women who had endured various degrees of custody loss. A book which explains the custody crisis in all of its crippling emotional complexity. A book that teaches parents ways to heal and how to help their children heal. But most of all, a book that would simply let all parents without custody know they are not alone in their grief.

This is the book I have written for you and other mothers and fathers. I believe it will help you survive your custody loss with hope—for yourself and your relationship with your children—intact.

Doreen Virtue
Lancaster, California

1

The Custody Crisis
What Is It?

*The really hard part is watching the boys go
home with their mother after a school event.
Why can't they go home with me? I'm their
father.*
   —Father without custody

When you, a divorcing parent, are faced with separation from your child, the emotional turmoil you go through is devastating. The separation itself is a real physical and emotional trauma. While the severity of the trauma depends partly on the age of your children, your relationship with them, and the custody decision by the court (for or against your wishes), the feelings generated by the breaking of the bond with your child are much like those after a loved one's unexpected death. The loss of day-to-day physical closeness with your child *hurts*. Many parents say they feel like an arm or leg has been lopped off. About the only initial reaction you can have to a trauma of this kind is shock. Then you go through a long period of stinging from the pain of the physical loss, enduring terrible sadness, confusion, and longing, and confronting what seems to be a spiritual void where the relationship with your child used to be.

  This is a time of extreme emotional upheaval. Divorce is always traumatic; breaking up a family adds another level of incredible stress. Consumed with feelings of grief, you mourn the loss of the parent-child relationship that is an inextricable part of the intact nuclear family. If you don't have primary custody, probably your first feeling is that you have lost your child forever. Another overwhelming feeling is fear—fear for the child's safety and well-being, fear of the loss of your child's love, and fear for your own sanity when these feelings overcome you.

What I have to tell you is good news: healing *is* possible. The custody crisis has hit your system like an earthquake, threatening the foundations of your life. However, this period of chaos will be followed by a time of thoughtful, careful rebuilding. My own experience, as well as the experiences of countless others who have gone through this before you, is positive evidence that you can become whole again. To actively mourn—to acknowledge your feelings deeply and accept them in order to gradually let them go—this is what is necessary to begin the healing and rebuilding process.

In her book, *Life Is Goodbye/Life Is Hello*, Dr. Alla Bozarth-Campbell describes the key moment in the healing process of a parent who is physically separated from his or her child: this is the moment when the parent comes to the realization that, physically, the child is "a truly separate being." Although the physical separation between you and your child was abrupt, forced, and may have happened too soon, it was, indeed, an inevitable part of bringing a unique human being into this world.

In healing emotionally, you weather a storm—a storm of damaged identity and violently negative feelings toward yourself and others. When the storm is spent, you are left with a pure sadness for what has been lost—continuous contact with the child—and a pure joy for what still remains—the child. Most importantly, you realize that physical distance does not have to equate with spiritual alienation. As Dr. Bozarth-Campbell tells us, "It is possible to be physically separated from someone, and spiritually united with him or her at the same time." You thus come to affirm the bond of love with the child, a bond that death, much less physical separation, cannot destroy. Throughout this painful period, the child still needs to be parented in the practical sense; the job of parenthood goes on, even if in a changed form.

This excruciating physical and emotional transition that you are going through is the process of grieving.

So, when we refer to the custody crisis, the word "crisis" doesn't refer to a short-term event or catastrophe, but rather to a lengthy personal journey. It begins when the loss of continuous contact with your child first becomes a threat, with that first thought of "what about the kids?" when divorce is initially discussed, when that first wave of anxiety wells up. From there, the custody crisis evolves into a spiral of emotions from bittersweet joy to utter defeat. It is a crisis that deeply shapes a parent's experiences and self-esteem. Though its intensity may diminish over time, the custody crisis is never over. Again, it simply changes form.

The notion that people go through certain stages in the process of grieving has been considered for some time. In his book, *The Grief Process*, Yorick Spiegel relates that many models for the grief cycle have been proposed over the years. In the early 1940s, Fulcomer distinguished four stages of grief: shock; "culturally patterned behavior controls"; "trial and error behavior"; and "repatterning." John Bowlby later identified three stages: "protest," "disorganization," and "reorganization."

In her book *On Death and Dying*, Dr. Elisabeth Kubler-Ross popularized the grief-stage concept, identifying five stages which terminal patients go through in grieving over their own impending death: denial and isolation; anger; bargaining; depression; and finally, acceptance. She notes that these are generally "the different stages that people go through when they are faced with tragic news—defense mechanisms in psychiatric terms, coping mechanisms to deal with extremely difficult situations."

For parents in the midst of a custody crisis, a five-stage model provides a convenient framework and springboard for understanding and recovering from their special kind of grief. In my work, I have come to use the following terms to describe the sequence of emotional, behavioral and thinking patterns associated with custody loss: shock; anger; panic; depression; acceptance. We will look at these stages in-depth in chapters 2 through 6. Included are many accounts of men and women who have lost, shared, or surrendered custody. In reading about their experiences, you will see that you are not alone. Often, discovering this is, in itself, very therapeutic. The stories, including my own, are real, although some details have been changed to protect privacy.

For some, if not most of us, feelings are difficult to identify and understand. This book is designed to help you become more aware of your feelings as well as possible reasons for them. The end of each chapter offers suggestions and techniques for dealing with your feelings in positive ways.

I have seen the five-stage grieving process operating in the lives of parents in hundreds of different situations. It seems that whatever the custody arrangements and regardless of *how* custody was lost, the emotions of shock, anger, panic and depression are present in varying degrees in most parents. Guilt and fear usually take their toll, in various forms, throughout the first four stages. The commonality of the experiences of the parents I've talked to is quite striking. But naturally, not everyone goes through each stage and not everyone goes through them in a particular order. The stages overlap, and while the shock stage, for example, may last a few weeks, the anger stage may literally go on for years and years. In addition, the amount of access to the child and the particular circumstances of the divorce and custody loss clearly do play a large part in determining the severity of any one parent's custody crisis. You will undoubtedly find that your own emotional pattern is unique and your own custody situation falls somewhere along a continuum between "total access to child/no access to child" and "custody taken away/willingly gave up custody."

This book speaks primarily to parents who are having to adjust to being separated from their children for significant periods of time. However, most-access parents—those with primary physical custody—also experience deep pain over custody issues and will benefit from looking at their own stages of grief. The most-access parent is frequently considered to be the "winner" in what, often, is a no-win situation. The custody crisis of a most-access parent consists of long lulls of normality, interspersed with temporary, and often fearful, periods of separation from the children. Just when things seem to be going smoothly, this parent has to relearn, once or twice per year or several times per year, what it feels like to send the children away. In many cases this is harder than the lot of the least-access parent, who makes, just once, but with terrible finality, the transition from full-time to part-time parent.

Pam, a patient of mine who has most-access custody, becomes very depressed every June when she sees her eight-year-old daughter depart by plane to visit her father in another state: "I cannot help but worry that I'll never see her again. I think her plane will crash or her dad will kidnap her or something. It makes me a basket case every summer!"

Another mother with primary custody poignantly summarized this pain. Her friend commented on the mother's having sent her boys off for their two-month yearly visitation with their father: "Free for two months, eh?'' The mother replied, ashen, ''Free, yes, and heartbroken.''

The *least-access* parent generally has contact with his or her children for a limited time such as summer, every other weekend, and holidays. The children may live hundreds of miles away, making spontaneous visits difficult or impossible. The least-access parent may have the freedom to make decisions about the child's daily life only during visitation periods.

Greg lost custody of his ten-year-old son and twelve-year-old daughter two years ago. He told me that when the kids leave him at the end of a visit, he aches as if he had lost custody just yesterday. He remains bitterly angry at his ex-wife: ''I just feel like she got everything and I got nothing. . . . She puts me through a great big hassle as if I don't have the right to see my own children.''

This situation constitutes, as I said, a considerable lifestyle change for the parent. We will explore ways to make this change later on. Positive communication skills will become vital in ensuring that the least-access parent has some input into the children's lives when they are with the most-access parent.

Then there is joint custody. This arrangement, also referred to as shared, split, or equal custody in different states, is based on the premise that children need a relationship with both parents following divorce. While it is still a fairly new custody arrangement, it has quickly taken over as the foremost type of custody. Presently, a majority of states have adopted joint-custody laws and it appears this trend will continue.

In most joint custody situations the child actually lives with one parent more than the other, spending time with the other parent on the weekends, during the summer, and/or other specific dates the parents or the judge decide upon. Joint or split custody becomes more complicated when parents live in different communities or states, and going between parents involves lengthy car or plane trips.

By current legal definition, all divorcing parents in states with joint custody laws share equally in custody unless the judge awards sole custody to one parent. This joint status could mean the children spend six months with one parent and six with the other; each parent may thus spend a significant part of his or her life with limited access to the children. This, too, requires considerable emotional readjustment.

For convenience, I'll be using the terms ''least-access'' and ''noncustodial'' interchangeably, as well as the terms ''most-access'' and "custodial." Of course, a parent with joint custody who sees his or her child only three months out of the year is technically custodial but actually least-access. And there are many other variations and special situations in custody settlements.

Many of us have wanted primary custody but lost. In the introduction, I described what I went through when I felt the ground was cut out from under me by the judge's decision. But voluntary surrendering of custody can be just as wrenching.

Georgia, a client of mine, left her husband, Frank, and gave him custody of their seven-year-old son, Dennis. "I didn't like being a mom," she said, "and I knew Frank would make a better parent for Dennis than I would." Georgia's parents harshly criticized her decision to surrender custody. Others refused to believe that she loved and still missed her son. Alone, miserable, and misunderstood, she finally sought therapy to put her self-image back together.

Some parents "volunteer" to surrender custody, feeling their chances of being awarded custody are slim. Others are judged legally unfit to retain custody. Feelings of guilt and unworthiness are particularly intense in these cases. There are also parents who initially had primary physical custody but later decided to relinquish custody for one reason or another. Joy, for example, didn't feel good about having her two children at the baby-sitter all day while she worked at her low-paying job. She reluctantly decided that her son and daughter would have a better life with her ex-husband and his new wife, a homemaker who could be home with the kids during the day. Another parent, Seth, also decided to give up custody even though he had gone through a long and expensive custody battle to have his daughter with him full-time. Seth's new wife, unaccustomed to having children around, was unable to adjust to having Seth's daughter living with them. This created problems in their marriage, causing them to argue and even contemplate divorce. Seth finally decided that this hostile atmosphere was unhealthy for everybody, and he relinquished custody of his daughter to his ex-wife.

To sum up, there are many different custody arrangements and there are innumerable reasons why people divorce and lose primary physical custody. In reading and using this book, as part of addressing the emotional pain brought on by losing regular contact with your children, you'll be reviewing your own story. This process includes finding ways to come to terms with your own part in what happened. Although this is not a book on coping with divorce (some excellent books on that subject are listed in the Suggested Reading section), throughout the book we'll explore ways to accept both what happened in the past and your current situation, and in doing so, prevent bitterness and regret from damaging your relationship with your kids.

In chapters 7 through 11, we will look at other issues accompanying custody loss—the external struggles that every parent involved with custody loss faces. Foremost among these challenges is keeping your relationship with your kids as close and loving as possible.

There is also the continuing relation with your ex-spouse. When children are involved in a divorce, there's no such thing as a complete separation from a former husband or wife. In fact, your ongoing relationship with your ex-spouse is extremely influential on how the divorce and custody arrangement will affect the children—a topic we will look at in depth in chapters 7 and 8.

We also tend to feel tremendous guilt when our own parents grieve over the loss of their grandchildren. It's heartbreaking to see your own parents grieve and feel that you're to blame. The custody crisis can throw your extended family out of balance, catapulting all of you into a fury of finger-pointing and blaming. This issue, too, will be discussed in a later chapter. We will consider, as well, the emotional ramifications of returning to court for another custody suit—a thought that has probably occurred to most of us at one time or another. Finally, we'll consider some of the stereotypes of mothers without custody and fathers without custody and discuss how to deal in a positive way with the prejudices of others.

In closing this chapter, I'd like to remind you that, in *On Death and Dying*, Dr. Kubler-Ross adds another element to the five stages of grief—"The one thing that usually persists through all these stages is hope." I have said that losing custody is like experiencing a death—the child is alive, but not always there; when the child leaves, the grieving begins again; when the child returns, it seems like a resurrection, and all your feelings, good and bad, arise as well. But hope is there, too: Your child needs you. Your child loves you. You will always be an important influence in that child's life.

Still, the road to the acceptance can be a long one. Let's travel it together.

2
When Our World
First Shatters: Shock

I felt like screaming, and I had an extremely hard time not just snapping at everyone. I really had to make an effort to keep calming myself down. I felt helpless and numb all at one time. One moment, I'd be crying, and the next moment, laughing.

> —Thirty-three-year-old mother of two, describing her reaction to hearing the judge award custody to her ex-husband

Shock. It's our initial reaction when we suffer a devastating loss. Even if we've anticipated that loss, when it finally occurs, we feel as though the world has viciously slapped us across the face. In this first stage of the custody crisis, we can only offer a bewildered "No, it just can't be true" as we struggle to believe that the kids really won't be living with us full-time anymore. It's important to remember that this feeling hits both parents who fought for custody and lost, and those who voluntarily surrendered custody.

Anita recalled how devastated she was one week after voluntarily giving up custody of her son and daughter: "You name it, I felt it. First there was the guilt. I felt so selfish and evil for giving up my kids, especially since they were just babies!"

She coughed and the tears, dammed up for so long, began to flow. She twisted a tiny tissue as she continued. "All I could think about at first was that I'd ruined their lives, and what kind of a horrible woman was I not to like being a mom?'' She paused and closed her eyes as if to shut out the pain reawakened by the recollection. "In my mind, I knew that it was better for the kids to be with Rick, but my emotions, plus everyone I knew, told me the opposite. I was a real mess for the first month or so, until I started listening to my true feelings instead of what everybody else was saying.''

Though Anita had known three months ahead of time that she was going to surrender custody, she was emotionally overwhelmed as well as caught off guard by the "how could you" reactions of others. She remained disoriented for about two months after she gave up custody.

Helen's custody loss, on the other hand, happened so suddenly that she had no time to prepare. Her ex-husband, bent on revenge following their divorce, reported to a social service agency that Helen was a heroin addict who couldn't care for her children. This wasn't true—she was not a drug addict—but within three days, her two small daughters were taken from their schools and placed in temporary foster homes pending an investigation.

She was beside herself, especially after learning that the girls had been sent to two different homes. "After it happened, I couldn't stop crying. I couldn't even do any work. My friends told me, 'Helen, you'll never get the kids back unless you snap out of this!' But I just couldn't stop crying!''

Numbed by the Onslaught of Emotions

While in the midst of shock, the first stage of your custody crisis, you may feel detached from the world, much like an astronaut suspended weightlessly above a space capsule. Images and words are slightly distorted by the time they reach your consciousness. Everything seems dull, and others may laugh at your absent-mindedness. You proceed through those first few days as if you're walking through a blanket of fog. It may be all you can do to get out of bed, go to work, and drag yourself home. Inside, you're struggling to break out of this waking coma. But you can't. Not yet. It's too painful.

You experience shock for good reasons. This feeling provides a layer of insulation against further emotional blows so that the reality of the loss can slowly sink in. It is a vital psychological cushion.

However, during those early days following custody loss, occasional realizations that your kids really *are* gone reach your conscious awareness. To me, these realizations were like the marbles in a pinball game that ricocheted unpredictably off different emotional "pins."

One moment you're numb, the next moment indignant about what your so-and-so ex-husband or wife did to you. But before you've felt the full impact of that rage, the next "marble" strikes and you sink into deep sorrow over thoughts of your children. Next you might find yourself whistling with relief that your marriage is finally over and you're free to move forward with your life.

Lose Yourself, Bury Your Grief

To cope with this flurry of feelings, parents often withdraw, burying themselves in some activity like cupboard straightening and lawn raking. Others turn to creative endeavors such as art or music that help them turn off the steady stream of self-recriminating and confusing thoughts hammering in their heads.

Twenty-eight-year-old Barbara, who works as a waitress, used reading to escape the pain she felt after losing custody of her son and daughter to her husband of eight years. "It started with one or two books every now and then, but lately I'm reading one book every two days," she said pointing to the huge fantasy-romance novel she was then reading. "I find they help me forget about the court case and keep me from worrying about the kids."

When Barbara lost custody, she too was totally unprepared. Her lawyer had promised that her case was solid, that she would get custody. "I had even told everyone at work that I'd get the kids," she recalled. But she didn't. The massive amount of reading she did was her way of licking her wounds. It was a period of hibernation for her; eventually, she curtailed the reading and was ready to re-enter the world a bit more.

Temporary escape into books, work, and hobbies can be a healthy way to deal with the initial pain of custody loss. Of course, if these pursuits are done to the exclusion of working or seeking friendships, they can exacerbate the custody crisis by creating other problems which then must be dealt with, even perhaps causing further grief, for instance, the loss of a friend or a job. In addition, if we use these activities to indefinitely avoid facing our feelings, resolution of our grief will never be achieved.

Mark, a sandy-haired grocery store clerk, is another patient who tried to lose himself and escape his feelings. But his choice of pursuits had traumatic results.

Though he'd had many doubts about whether he'd get custody, Mark had held steadfastly to the hope that the judge would see he was the better parent. After all, he was the one who would stay home with the children when they were sick. Mark also fixed most of the meals. Not Gail, his wife—she was "always working," he said. So when the judge ruled in Gail's favor, Mark was bitterly disappointed. He was also numbed by the accusations Gail's lawyer had made that Mark was an abusive father, and by the stern lecture the judge gave Mark about positive parenting. The support and visitation schedule the judge subsequently outlined made Mark feel faint and sick to his stomach. "Couldn't the judge see that Gail was lying? How could he lecture me about parenting, when it was Gail who needed lessons on how to care for children? It all seemed so unreal."

In the weeks that followed his custody loss, Mark drank heavily and stalked women. He later said, "What I was really doing was trying to boost my ego. I met each of these really cute chicks in this bar where some of my friends used to go. Yeah, Gloria, Penny, and Cindy . . . with each of them I thought, 'This is gonna be it.' But instead I ended up feeling disgusted with myself 'cause they turned out to be more messed up in their heads than I was."

Rebounding into a sexual relationship (or several different relationships) is another way of trying to lose ourselves. But, as in Mark's case, this frequently gets us embroiled in yet another emotionally wrenching and draining situation. Every one-night stand, every aborted "whirlwind romance," is another kind of loss. You don't need another one of those at this point in the custody crisis.

Mark attempted to drown his anguish in alcohol and romance; Janet, a thirty-six-year-old noncustodial mother, tried to use food. Every evening after work, she'd go home and eat whatever was around. It wasn't long before she gained twenty-five pounds. Janet recognized she was eating to escape, but she felt unable to control herself. "Right at that time in my life," she said, "I was using food because I couldn't handle my emotions. You name it, I was going through it right then—guilt, being angry, missing my kids and just not feeling very good about myself at all. Eating kept me from facing those feelings.''

I Haven't Been Myself Lately

When people are in shock, they may manifest a marked change in behavior; they can be moody, impulsive and unpredictable. At a time when he or she needs support and love the most, the parent may be abandoned by people who don't understand how shock creates erratic and alienating behavior. Or the parent may become withdrawn. Others become highly dependent on their own parents or friends to take care of them.

One mother recalled how she dissolved into tears almost every day at work for one month after she lost custody. Another grew increasingly cynical and seemed to be aching for a fight with everyone she knew after a judge ordered her to share joint custody with her ex-husband. After surrendering custody of his kids to his ex-wife, one father reported that he became rigid and overbearing at work, demanding unrealistically high standards of performance from his employees.

Regression to an immature state of mind and behavior is also common. For a time, emotion, not logic, governs the parent. It stands to reason if you're in a daze, you will probably be careless toward others at times; this can leave permanent scars on relationships.

Few of Kim's co-workers have forgotten her behavior after she lost custody of her daughter. Her inconsistent work habits left a bitter aftertaste among those who had to take up the slack. Kim felt guilty once she recovered from the shock and her work stabilized, but she still sees evidence that those first two months following her custody loss deeply affected her position at work. The respect and admiration she previously felt has been replaced by distrust: "Looking back at it now, it was like I was someone else during that time. I was just in such a daze after Nicole went to live with my ex, and I can't really remember everything I did or said back then. The only way I know that I blew it at work so badly is from what everyone tells me, and the way they've treated me so differently since that time."

Without realizing it, during those first weeks or months after custody loss, parents may also project their feelings onto other people. This, too, is normal. Barbara, the waitress who buried herself in romance novels, also projected as a means of coping. While undergoing the custody proceedings, she had assured her co-workers over and over that she would retain custody. However, when her ex-husband was given custody, instead of acknowledging her own pain, Barbara said she felt "like I let the other waitresses down by not getting custody of my kids."

Barbara, of course, was the one who was hurt and disappointed, not her co-workers, although they were probably very sympathetic to her situation. The realization of just exactly what had occurred dawned on Barbara very slowly. And when she was ready to acknowledge the profound disappointment she was feeling, she stopped projecting her feelings onto her friends and claimed them as her own. Most of us are like Barbara; we stop projecting as the reality of our situation becomes evident and we acknowledge just how much it hurts to be separated from our kids.

Related to projection is the fact that many of us spend those first few weeks or months thinking about reasons why we are not responsible for the custody situation, or insisting against all facts in our case that we will somehow regain full custody. This denial is not necessarily wrong; it's another initial reaction to unbearable emotional baggage. To accept responsibility doesn't feel possible when you can hardly accept that you have lost anything in the first place. When terribly stressful, unpleasant, and/or tragic events occur in our lives, denial is sometimes the only thing that allows us to keep functioning somewhat normally.

But the insidious thing about all these perfectly normal reactions which occur when we are in shock is that they engulf us at a stage when we're supposed to be making crucial decisions that could affect both ourselves and our children for the rest of our lives. Instead of carefully weighing choices, we are overwhelmed by confusion and stress. We shut down. We can't hear, see, or think clearly. Too many stimuli. Too much to bear. Our powers of concentration are impaired and we are forgetful. Worst of all, we can't find a way to snap out of it.

Shock is almost impossible to shake off through conscious effort alone. At this stage you may feel like your life will never be stable or serene again. But time is the friend of the newly noncustodial parent. The fog *does* gradually lift.

Hidden Pain

Some parents who are new to lost or split custody appear to handle the whole thing just fine, remaining their old efficient selves at work, going calmly through the legal proceedings, and prompting others to comment, "Look how strong he is" or "What a cold-hearted woman—she doesn't seem upset in the least that she's lost her kids." Of course, such appearances may camouflage a deeply troubled person who feels unable to reveal his or her shock and pain to others.

This is exactly what happened to me following my custody loss. On my first day without the boys, I walked to my college classes, unaware of my surroundings, my feelings, even my own self. It was as though I were peering at the world through a tiny porthole. Yet, I kept my chin high and an "everything's fine" smile plastered on my face.

After my first class, I met privately with my psychology professor. A strict member of the behaviorist school of thought, she wasn't much for talking about feelings. "Well, Doreen," she said, "you can expect your grades to take a real nose-dive while you're going through the divorce and struggling over custody of your children. After all, you won't be able to concentrate on your studies while you're in a personal crisis."

Though her statement was intended to ease my worries about school, I interpreted it as a glove slapping me across the face and challenging me to a duel. I made a mental note to, if anything, improve my grades.

The rest of that day I drifted in a fog, not feeling the cement under my feet as I walked to my classes. I felt waves of relief that my marriage was finally over. But that was followed by another wave of panic, believing that now I had nothing. No one. My children were gone and I was completely alone. I could feel my stomach wrench, as if the earth had opened up below me and I was falling into a bottomless hole.

Chuck and Grant. My sons—were they okay? I looked at my watch and knew they were probably home with their father right now. I wondered if they were crying for me. As I headed toward my last class, I felt trapped. I knew that I had had no choice but to end the marriage. But the kids . . . I played back all my reasons for sending them back to their father, looking for anything I may have missed that would have allowed me to keep them. The regrets had begun.

I was on an emotional roller coaster and beginning to lose my grip. I walked over to the college counseling office. The receptionist asked me what I wanted. As she led me into the counselor's office, I floated behind her, unsure of what I *did* want from the counselor.

"I just got a divorce," I heard myself blurt out to the counselor. I hoped she'd know what I needed.

"I'm sorry," the counselor said, "but it's registration time and all we can do is help you decide on a class schedule. We can't help you with personal problems until after February."

Why was it that, twice that day, two helping professionals hadn't helped me? Where was the support of my friends when I needed it most? Part of my problem was that I didn't really ask for help. Something prevented me from showing the world and admitting to myself that I felt tormented. Since I seemed okay, others assumed I was okay.

On an intellectual level, I knew that I was without my kids, but I thought I just had to blink my eyes and change the situation any time I wanted, as easily as switching television stations. I did not see that with each month my children stayed with their father, I would have an increasingly difficult time regaining custody. The next five months were to contain a series of small decisions that added up to a devastating reality: me without my sons.

During the next few months, I went home and climbed into my reading assignments where it was safe and I could forget the world. That semester I got the highest grades in all my classes.

I had shut down and died emotionally. That was my own personal style of being in shock.

First Steps toward Healing

During the initial period of separation, you may feel as though your children have left you forever. Their voices and laughter echo in your mind, and it feels very strange to know that those sounds aren't really coming from the children. You discover how odd it feels to come home from work and find the children aren't there, or to drive past the baby-sitter's house and not stop to pick up the kids. All your old routines change, compelling you to constantly remind yourself, "Oh yeah, that's right, the kids aren't here." Everything, from what you buy at the grocery store to what you watch on TV, is drastically altered immediately after the kids stop living with you. But there is a considerable time lag between their leaving and your becoming accustomed to a childless lifestyle. The sadness that accompanies each realization that "my kids don't live with me anymore" can be truly incapacitating.

But you will see your children again. The reality is that at this moment your kids are engaging in their routine activities of meals, baths, and homework. You just can't peek into their rooms and see them at will anymore. But you'll still be in their thoughts, and you will make a big impact on their lives regardless of your custody status. Your relationship will continue in some different—but equally special—way.

No matter how alone and confused you feel now, rest assured that it is a *temporary* feeling. Remember that shock's purpose is to provide cushioning for our fragile inner selves as we prepare to accept what we once considered unacceptable. So, instead of trying to avoid or escape our feelings, we can find ways to make this period in the custody crisis more comfortable.

First, *tell the important people in your life what you're going through.* Explain that your custody situation has left you in shock and that your behavior may seem odd or inappropriate at times. Tell them that you'll do your best to deal with it, but that you may need time to feel like your old self again. Of course, you'll want to avoid a lengthy saga of your divorce and custody loss with people with whom you aren't close. By broaching the subject and being sensitive to the reactions of others, however, you may find that your co-workers and friends have gone through similar experiences. This type of support can be very comforting.

Secondly, ask yourself who among your friends and relatives are good listeners. Don't be afraid of seeming weak or dependent. Rather, approach your friends with your adult needs for support. Tell them that you are feeling confused right now, and ask if they would mind if you talked some things through. If they are sensitive, they will recognize this for the genuine crisis it is.

However, you may not have access to people who are willing or ready to just listen to you. Some people who genuinely want to help may be confused when you express one feeling on Monday and the opposite feeling on Tuesday; they don't understand the nature of shock. Or you may find that others try to "rescue" you or solve your problems for you instead of just allowing you to vent your feelings. You may even find yourself trying to comfort others who become upset when you tell them about your grief. And there's the risk of damaging a friendship by leaning on one person too long and too hard during your time of need. For these reasons, mental health resources such as a therapist or support group can provide helpful, guilt-free comfort. Suggestions for contacting and utilizing these services are described in chapter 5.

Thirdly, be aware of your own words and actions. Watch for potentially irritating and offensive behavior toward others. But don't kick yourself for such behavior when it does occur; it is a normal part of what you are going through. Be gentle with yourself. If your feelings start to seem uncontainable, it is perfectly acceptable to excuse yourself, leave the room, and seek solitude in which to cool off or sort things out.

Perhaps the most important way to help yourself during this time, and throughout the custody crisis, is to become more aware of your feelings instead of trying to block them out. Honestly acknowledging your internal state ("I'm feeling sad right now," "I can't see any answers right now") provides enormous relief. It increases your sense of control and self-respect, because your feelings, however harsh, changeable, or muddled, are important, and they are not wrong. Tuning in to how you feel also lessens the periods of absolutely overwhelming emotional pain, making it harder for such feelings to sneak up on you in times of stress.

Here is one way to practice beginning or increasing awareness of your feelings:

—Find a quiet place to sit alone in a comfortable position. There should be no distractions, including time limits. Take the phone off the hook and put a "do not disturb" sign on the door if you have to.

—With eyes closed, take three or four slow, deep breaths. As you exhale each time, feel your muscles start to unwind and relax, one by one. Spend a while thinking about, picturing and feeling all the muscles of your body and relaxing them, one by one.

—Let your mind wander in any direction. Don't try to control your thoughts in any way. Become part of your thoughts, not merely an observer of them.

—Do not criticize or edit your thinking process. Do not think in terms of right and wrong. You don't have to analyze your feelings, chart their course, justify them, like or dislike them. Just feel them.

—As the mind wanders, be aware of any bodily changes (tightening muscles, fluttering in the stomach, changes in heart rate).

—When you're done (this could be when you feel tired, are finished thinking about a certain subject or just want to stop), review your thoughts. What was their theme: worry? wanting to have more control and say-so over yourself, or other people or circumstances? anger? exhaustion? guilt?

—Remember whatever bodily changes occurred. What was their pattern? Did your stomach feel different when you thought of a certain subject? Are your muscles more relaxed or less relaxed than before you began the exercise?

—Try to describe these emotional and physical sensations in words. Do they feel warm, cold, soft, sharp, pleasant, frightening, or perhaps all mixed together? How do you feel as you begin to identify these different feelings?

—Finally, take a few moments to think about the reasons for your present feelings. This is not a formal analysis; you are not trying to solve anything or get to the bottom of anything. Rather, you are trying to see *connections*. Do your feelings have to do with fears? Are they fears you haven't thought consciously about before? What are your deepest fears? Do they stem from self-doubt? Are you disturbed by something someone else said? Why might a particular remark have hit you the way it did? Forget the motives and problems of other people; you cannot control them anyway. Think about your own feelings. On the positive side, are you giving yourself enough credit for your accomplishments, for having tried, for having done your best in a given situation? Have you practiced self-forgiveness?

Make the time to practice this self-awareness technique often.

There are many other things you can do to increase relaxation and centeredness. Regular exercise is a must! Other ways are getting a massage, enjoying a sauna, participating in a team sport, practicing yoga or other meditation techniques, biofeedback, and playing with pets. It may be that you have been meaning to start exercising or to investigate one of these options or another option.

Now, at the beginning of your custody crisis, may seem the most inappropriate or even bizarre time to start doing these things. So often in our culture we feel guilty when we take time for ourselves to relax and feel good. It goes against our programming that constantly says, "Be productive." But consider this—you will not resolve your grief by wandering in a daze, ignoring your feelings, and remaining off balance. And your productivity—whatever "productivity" means for you as a social and spiritual being—will be severely curtailed if you do not work gently through your grief.

You don't have to go through custody loss "the hard way." You deserve to be happy regardless of your custody status.

3
Waking Up Angry

I feel so much pressure now, and I can't stand it! My parents and friends are always on me to "Get the kids back! Get the kids back!" Man, it makes me so mad the way everyone's on my case about the kids. It seems like I've been this angry for this last whole month! In fact, I can't ever remember being so angry for so long.

　　　—Twenty-four-year-old woman,
　　　　five months after surrendering
　　　　custody of her children

Barry was still in shock nearly a month after his wife of thirteen years left with their two daughters. He is a thirty-seven-year-old financial planner. "I was so numb," he recalls, "that it felt like I was sleep-walking." Though Cindy and the girls had taken most of the furniture and all of their personal belongings, Barry continued to believe during that first month after they left that his family would return for a joyful reconciliation. It wasn't until a deputy sheriff handed him a divorce summons that the thought bolted through his mind: "My God, will I ever see my daughters again?"

Still disbelieving that his family was really gone, Barry called on a friend for comfort. But instead, what he got was some sound advice: "Get a lawyer—fast." Though still unconvinced that Cindy was serious about the divorce, Barry contacted and retained an attorney.

Three days later, Barry received a large envelope in the mail from Cindy's lawyer. Inside was a one-hundred item questionnaire on topics ranging from Barry's sex life to his financial status.

Suddenly, Barry felt panic and anger. His chest tightened and heat rose from his neck to his face. He was instantly on the phone to his lawyer. "I'm sorry, he's away from his desk," the receptionist answered. When his attorney hadn't returned his message after two hours, Barry left another message. After awhile he left another.

He still hadn't heard from his attorney a day and a half later when he received a second, more frightening form from Cindy's attorney. At that point, he decided to visit his lawyer in person. When the receptionist told him the attorney was out of town for three days, Barry became unglued. He unleashed the hostility which had been building for some time—in a verbal sledgehammer aimed at the receptionist. When she began to cry, Barry suddenly stopped and became angry at himself. He mumbled embarrassed apologies and hurried out of the office.

Barry's wife and kids had left without warning. They had taken many of his cherished possessions, including his beloved cocker spaniel, Goldie. They had also taken away his role of husband and father. His attorney was ignoring his messages. His anger was legitimate. His choice of targets was unfortunate.

Without Custody and Furious

I would say that generally, the cold facts of custody loss aren't fully realized until about two to four months following the beginning of the crisis. It's like waking from a nightmare to find that the monster is still there—really there. Then comes the scream of protest, "NO! This can't be happening to me!" The red hot, impatient anger of the custody crisis has set in.

At first it's generalized anger—just plain mad, all the time. The strength and suddenness of this emotion can take you by surprise. Michelle shocked herself when she flew into a rage and threw her iron to the floor with all her might after it dripped rusty water on the blouse she'd been ironing. Before her decision to allow her eleven-year-old son to live with his father, Michelle had always been very quiet and even-tempered. She was bewildered and frightened by her own outbursts.

Within a short time, generalized anger such as Michelle's gives way to anger over specific issues, as the custody trial and subsequent custody arrangements unfold.

Frequently, we feel during this crisis that our personal rights are being violated. Perhaps false accusations are made during the custody trial. Or we disagree with how the judge arrives at a decision about custody, visitation or support. There are countless instances between the moment divorce is first contemplated and the time custody arrangements are determined when we will feel victimized by an ex-spouse, lawyers, relatives, and the judicial system. From our feelings of helplessness erupts seething anger.

We also direct anger toward ourselves. We kick ourselves for doing this or saying that, believing that we committed some fatal mistake which led to custody loss. Parents who voluntarily surrender custody are just as, if not more, susceptible to self-inflicted punishment.

Drew was a parent whose self-directed anger was intense. He had initiated the divorce when his wife's realty business began booming. "I regret the way I handled the whole situation. All I wanted was to get more attention from my wife, not a divorce. It's just that she was spending ten- and twelve-hour days at the office! I just got fed up and overreacted." He hung his head and tried to conceal the tear he wiped with the back of his hand.

When Drew asked for primary physical custody of his nine-year-old son, his lawyer assured him he was a shoo-in. However, on the day of the trial, the judge disappeared into his chambers with both divorce lawyers; when they reappeared, the decisions surrounding Drew's case had been completed. Drew was horrifed to learn that Carol was to retain custody and Drew was ordered to pay four hundred dollars a month child support and four hundred dollars a month alimony.

"When I heard the judge's decision, I almost passed out," Drew bitterly recalled. "Then I thought, 'Now you've really screwed yourself! Not only did you lose your wife and son, now you're in a tight money bind.'" As Drew's anger and guilt mounted, he searched desperately for a way to redeem his sense of self, his relationship with his son, and his financial problems. But Carol was an obstacle to all three of these hopes. He began to fantasize about having Carol murdered. "Divorce makes you crazy!" he cried during one session. "I hit bottom with my thinking and emotions when I wanted to have Carol killed. I kept thinking that if she were dead, I wouldn't have to pay alimony or child support, and then I'd get my son back. I never came close to doing anything about it—I'm sure I never could—but the thoughts of murder showed me how stressed I was.''

Violent thoughts, directed toward ourselves or others, are actually rather common and are generally no cause for alarm. I've found that most people have brutal fantasies, from time to time, about loved ones being killed or maimed. It is estimated that eighty percent of us have thought about what it would be like to commit suicide. But since it's not common knowledge that almost everyone has thoughts like these, we feel a lot of shame and guilt about them. Once they admit to having these thoughts, my patients frequently ask, "Do these thoughts mean that I wish my ex-spouse (or myself, my children, my parents) were dead?," "Does this mean I could lose control and actually cause harm to them or myself?" and "If they do die, would it be because of my thoughts about their deaths?" The answer to all of these is no. Fantasy is not reality.

But a word of caution is in order: if these violent thoughts ever seem to be out of hand and beckoning you to take action on them, please pick up the phone and call the nearest hospital, mental health professional, physician, or other emergency aid. If in doubt about your impulse control, don't hesitate to ask for guidance.

Anger is also a manifestation of pain. We become combative because the world has treated us cruelly. We behave like any creature who hurts and believes that he is his only protection from a hostile environment. But of course, there are sources of protection for us. Our animosity is a normal and temporary part of our grief.

Anger fulfills several purposes in a crisis. First, it allows us time to slowly face, through a different kind of smokescreen, these inevitable truths: "I am somewhat (or completely) responsible for what is happening or what has happened," and "The loss really has occurred."

Second, and very importantly, anger propels us into action. Divorce cases, custody suits or mediations, and the protection of visitation rights in uncontested custody suits require enormous amounts of energy and endurance. At some point we think, "I'm not going to just sit around here and cry, I'm going to *do* something!" When it leads to constructive action, anger is empowering and energizing in the first stages of the crisis. When it is self-directed or directed at irrelevant and/or innocent targets (remember Barry screaming at the hapless receptionist), it is destructive, draining, and prohibitive to growth and healing. But more on that later.

Third, anger often forces us to vent our feelings. How many times have you seen someone raging over something, and then break down and weep? Anger is often a cover-up for sorrow, fear, hurt, loneliness, jealousy, insecurity and many other emotions, because anger is a more socially acceptable emotion (especially for men). It's often the one emotion both men and women show when we can't hold in everything.

Triggers for Anger

At this stage, we sometimes feel almost like a puppet, unpredictably controlled by our own anger. Anger can be triggered by something as insignificant as a friend's offhand remark about your custody status, or as important as your ex-spouse deliberately making the children unavailable for your appointed visitation period. We will talk about ways to handle anger at the end of this chapter. But first let's look more specifically at what's making us so mad. Least-access and most-access parents always seem to have their own special complaints, but many anger triggers are reported by parents who share custody in any way. To begin to deal with your anger, try to identify which of the following general categories are the ones that consistently set you off. Don't be surprised if you find that many or most of them do. Just reading down this list, plus writing in your own anger triggers, will give you an idea of the amount of stress the custody crisis involves.

Least-Access Parents:

Access to the children is now severely limited. Obviously, anger over this issue is particularly intense among parents who involuntarily lose custody. You must now live by the visitation schedule arranged by a judge or mediator, a schedule that may limit visitations with your children to every other weekend and alternating holidays. As a noncustodial parent, you resent losing that daily contact, those small details of the child's life. The triumphant grin after earning an "A" in math. The cozy and impromptu intimacy of watching a scary movie together on a Saturday afternoon. Instead, you may have to learn to be content with, and make the best of, sharing much of the children's lives at a distance.

You feel no control over how the children are raised. Least-access parents' anger is often related to feeling that they have minimal input in forming their children's values. It's a concern even among parents with joint custody who stand by helplessly as ex-spouses intentionally or unintentionally fail to consult them before selecting children's schools, churches, physicians. They are your children, too, and yet your opinions and values about what's best for them may seem to carry little weight.

You sense that the children are neglected despite child support payments. What noncustodial parent hasn't worried whether the kids are getting enough to eat and have proper clothes and shoes? It's hard to shut off such worries when you once supervised your child's well-being on a daily basis. But worry turns to fury when you conscientiously send hundreds of dollars in support each month, only to find that some of the children's important wants or needs are being inadequately met. "What the hell is that money for?" you wonder. And you may really seethe with the suspicion that the money is being used by your ex-spouse to enhance his or her social life.

You feel that your dreams related to the kids are shattered. Ed always imagined his son, Edward Jr., would take over his contracting business someday. But when his ex-wife Sharon remarried and moved with little Ed to another state, Ed Sr. was devastated. "I don't stand a chance of making a dent in my own son's life now that Sharon and that Bill character she married have him under their control," he complained. "Bill even has the gall to make Ed call him Dad!"

When the role of "traditional" parent is taken away following custody loss, many of us feel that a chunk of our identities has been lost. A substantial portion of our lives, and of our sense of the future, may have centered around the children.

Most-Access Parents:

You fear for the children's safety and well-being when they go for visitations. Maureen cringed as she watched her ex-husband's car pull out of the driveway. Inside, she could see the tops of the heads of her three small children in the back seat. Each time Jerry took the kids for a weekend, Maureen worried about the hour-long drive ahead of them. She remembered how erratically he used to drive when they were married. Maureen eventually asked Jerry if she could deliver the children to his house on Friday nights and pick them up on Sundays. This helped reduce her fears, but she still had to block out thoughts of Jerry driving the kids around while they were with him.

We all worry about our children when they're out of earshot and eyesight. These fears are usually only alleviated when we trust the caretaker who has the children. After a bitter divorce and custody dispute, many ex-spouses are not in an emotional position to trust one another.

You fear the children won't be returned. Many a most-access parent has experienced the gripping fear of waiting for his or her child to be returned from a visit—and then the clock keeps ticking and the ex-spouse doesn't show up. A consistently late drop-off is a serious violation of the court order and you should probably take legal action if it happens on more than three occasions within a short period of time. Before that, however, try talking to your ex-spouse about it (see chapter 8).

It's scary enough to see your child go off accompanied by someone you don't fully trust. Someone you know would love to have custody of the child. Someone who may have lied and used deception in court. Most-access parents often have the sinking feeling they may never see their child again. They feel helpless against a court order that says they must let the other parent see the child on a regular basis.

Your ex-spouse fails to pay child support or always pays late. As a most-access parent, you may feel like you are raising the children while the least-access parent gets a "free ride"—that is, the ability to enjoy the fun times with the child while you get the job of maintaining discipline and teaching the children personal responsibility. You may also feel overburdened by the everyday financial strains that accompany raising a child. School supplies, clothing, toys and entertainment cost a lot of money.

When child support payments are late or absent, most-access parents go through a variety of reactions from panic to disgust. Certainly, there are legal channels which force "deadbeat dads" and "deadbeat moms" to make good on their obligations, but these can seem frustratingly slow. And it's illegal to refuse visitation rights because child support hasn't been paid, unless it's backed up with a court order.

Parents Who Share Custody in Any Way:

There is a new person in your ex-spouse's life. You may be threatened by the role of a new lover or spouse, especially if your ex has primary custody. You realize that this person may have a profound influence over your children in the years to come. This fear and anger is intense if the new stepparent or lover has values significantly contrary to yours.

Your ex-spouse does or says things you dislike. I'll never forget the night I picked my boys up from my ex-husband's house and found that he had given them a "buzz"—that is, shaved off most of their hair. I took one look at their quarter-inch-long hair and couldn't help but let out a shriek of horror. The best I could do was to contact my lawyer and ask him to talk to my ex-husband's lawyer about preventing it in the future.

When children go from one parent's home to another, one or both parents may use them to try to get even with each other by waging a slander campaign or long distance argument. The children may appear brainwashed as they recount stories told to them by the other parent, or by a stepparent. When this happens, it's tempting to counter with, "Well, just let me tell you what Mommy or Daddy did before you were born!" But of course, it's the child who suffers the most by being in the middle of these tattle-tale wars.

You must endure the financial setbacks of divorce, custody suit and custody sharing. Before his wife left with their two daughters, Phil was proud that he had managed to save five thousand dollars over several years. Two months after reaching that financial goal, his passbook balance was $530. Not only had Barbara withdrawn half the money, but the lawyer he hired to fight for custody required a retainer fee of fifteen hundred dollars. Phil also had to pay the insurance deductible for psychological evaluations of the entire family—something Phil's lawyer assured him was necessary.

As Phil discovered, the cost of a custody battle can be overwhelming—often ranging from a minimum of five thousand dollars to upwards of twenty thousand dollars. This, unfortunately, places many parents out of the running in any potential chance they'd have in retaining or regaining custody. So, for many, the idea of having custody is little more than a dream along the lines of owning a sports car or winning the lottery. It seems out of reach, but is still the subject of continual longing.

Most-access parents, particularly mothers, also usually experience a drastic reduction in income after the dust from the divorce and custody dispute has settled. In fact, a recent study conducted by the University of Michigan reported that mothers with custody experience an average income decrease of fifty percent following divorce. Noncustodial fathers, on the other hand, often experience a rise in their standard of living due to decreased expenses. It is estimated that almost half the families headed by single women live below the federally-determined poverty line. To add to this financial strain and emotional stress, little more than half of all most-access parents (men and women) receive child support payments from their ex-spouses.

You have to put up with the inconveniences of sharing custody. In addition to the financial devastation of custody loss, there are a thousand little nuisances which arise, and they, as much as anything else, trigger anger. Visitation may involve miles of driving or lengthy airplane flights. Lots of packing and unpacking. Trying to arrange for baby-sitting during those short periods when work overlaps with visitation can be frustrating and embarrassing as one tries to explain to the sitter why the job will last only a week, a month, or a summer.

You must cope with the red tape and insensitivity of the legal system. For many of us, the custody trial may be our first up-close experience with the legal system. Anger may sprout from misunderstanding the mechanics of the system and thus feeling powerless and afraid. It's overwhelming to realize that total strangers can control your life. You're taken aback when you must stand mute before a judge and listen to your personal life being publicly rehashed. The criteria used to determine who will get custody may seem illogical or inappropriate. The judge may appear to make sweeping decisions without really knowing all the facts involved. Attorneys may be patronizing and inaccessible. It can be a disillusioning nightmare.

You see your children and their grandparents devastated by the divorce and custody dispute. As parents, we face a basic dilemma when we contemplate a divorce and custody suit: Is it worth the emotional toll it takes on the child? We think, "Maybe I should just give up custody instead of dragging Johnny through a court case," or "This whole, stupid battle is just putting the kids through hell for no good reason!"

In addition, to press on with the suit, and/or to lose custody, often means seeing our own parents suffer tremendous pain. When Karen lost custody of her young son Jeremy, her mother's reaction took her by surprise. "Mom cried for days," Karen recalled. "I felt so guilty, but I couldn't admit that to myself for a long time. Instead, I took it out on my ex-husband!"

Take some time to elaborate on the specifics of your situation for each of the above categories and/or add some of your own anger triggers. As part of your increasing awareness of your feelings, chart the course of your anger. What makes you mad, when, and why? Often, of course, you won't know why. But try looking for patterns. This will help you plan to deal with your anger assertively (see the end of the chapter).

Slinging Arrows

As we recover from shock and pass into this second stage of the custody crisis, we commonly go on a vengeful hunt for someone or something we can blame for our misery. We try to dole out some of our pain to others. Ex-spouses, parents, and attorneys are the favored targets. This unloading of anger and hurt comes in the form of "If it weren't for you, none of this would have happened!"

Mostly, the real issues underlying these assaults are, "I hurt and cannot deal with it right now," "I feel overwhelmed and need to feel that someone else is responsible and will make everything okay for me," and "I am afraid that I will not be able to fix things on my own, that I will fail (or I have failed) and will lose my children forever and it will be all my fault if I do."

Friends and relatives may be bullied into taking these angry explanations to heart and believe that they are somehow responsible for the custody situation. When this occurs, the friend or relative may try to resolve or reduce the conflict by "rescuing" the parent— an action they invariably regret in the long run.

Julie was able to hook her parents into taking blame for her divorce and custody loss with disastrous results. As I got to know Julie, it became clear that she was accustomed to blaming others for her life circumstances. She did not like to make decisions, preferring instead to let life make choices for her. She had married and had three children within two and a half years. She sensed that her life lacked joy, and ascribed this lack to a faceless force she called "them" or "they." In her mind, Julie was a victim and "they" were the perpetrators.

> Ron and I broke up because we never had any time to ourselves. We couldn't afford a baby-sitter, so I'd always ask my mom and dad to watch the kids for us. All we wanted to do was maybe go to a movie or something. But, do you think my folks would ever watch the kids? No. I can't believe how selfish my parents were! It's all their fault. If they had been willing to baby-sit, Ron and I would still be together.

Julie, without a job or any money to support herself, surrendered custody of her two sons and daughter to her ex-husband and moved in with her parents the next day. For the first few weeks, Julie was quiet and withdrawn. She stayed mostly in her bedroom watching television during the day. But soon the yelling and accusations began. Julie believed the divorce and custody loss were her parents' fault, and she didn't hesitate to tell them so. She screamed it, hollered it, bellowed it. Her parents finally—partly in desperation and partly out of habit formed while Julie was growing up—accepted responsibility.

So, anxious to alleviate the fairly hefty guilt they felt, they catered to Julie's every whim. Her father hired an attorney for her. Her mother did laundry, made special meals, and ran her errands. Sadly, by trying to do everything possible to make Julie smile and feel better, all three grew despondent, sullen, and bitter. Eventually, her parents grew resentful of her.

Julie also grew more miserable with each favor her parents did. Inside, she ached to take charge of her own life but was too frightened to do so. She had never really risked doing something on her own, and she was certain that if she attempted anything big, anything important, she would surely fail. Julie's parents were robbing her of the opportunity to succeed through trial and error, which is the way most of us have to make our way.

Newly noncustodial parents should be alert to their own attempts to blame others and vent their anger in ways that manipulate and hurt other people. Remember, your ex-spouse, the children, the new girlfriend or boyfriend, various attorneys and psychologists, the legal system, the whole world—none of these is exclusively responsible for your custody situation. Again, it will help for you to openly express your pain to your loved ones; explain that the frustrations of your custody situation make it tempting for you to lash out, but you're practicing healthy ways to deal with your anger.

Coming to Terms with Child Support Payments

Child support payments are the bane of most noncustodial parents. Every month, the check that must be signed and mailed is a stressful reminder of least-access status—a reminder that "not only did I lose the kids, but now I have to pay money for not having them."

Tears of frustration and rage may well up in the hardiest of parents who feel they should get something for their money. The payments can feel like a life sentence, with no end in sight. Many of us, especially those who left the marriage and initiated the divorce, feel angry toward ourselves for creating the conditions that resulted in support payments.

Drew, the noncustodial father who fantasized about murdering his ex-wife, recovered from his anger and self-recrimination by learning to look at his financial situation differently: "I have finally stopped looking at what I don't have and have started focusing on what I do have." There is a great deal of wisdom in this statement. Drew realized that it is futile to worry about things that cannot be changed. He understood that unless he was willing to return to court and attempt a reduction or elimination of child support payments, getting angry was not going to lead anywhere. Drew chose to look for some good in a situation beyond his control.

And there is a lot of good in paying child support. Providing money to ensure that the children have enough food, clothing, and shelter can be seen as an act of love, not a sign of surrender to the enemy camp. The children did not ask for the divorce and they should not have to suffer for it. Least-access parents must remember that they will always be their children's mother or father regardless of whom the children live with. And being a parent means certain financial obligations. The child support payment system was established to ensure that children's needs are met by both parents and is not intended as punishment for or revenge against the noncustodial parent.

"But what if I'm paying child support and it's not being used for the children?" is a common protest. It certainly is frustrating to have children report to you that some aspect of their care or leisure time which you think is important is not being paid for by your ex-spouse. However, if it's apparent the children are eating well, have adequate shelter, proper medical care, competent baby-sitters and seemingly appropriate clothing (ascertained by asking the children, dropping by their primary residence, or talking to their teachers or baby-sitters), it can be assumed that the child support check is being used legitimately. If you still suspect your payments are being squandered, you should first consult your ex-spouse. Often a simple explanation is possible. If this doesn't yield satisfactory results, seek legal advice.

Anger and Aggression

Anger is an important part of the grieving process; the word "anger" comes from an Old Norse word, *angr*, meaning "grief and sorrow." But if anger is to facilitate the grieving process, you need to focus on how best to express your anger. Will your anger be expressed in destructive ways or communicated through positive means which lead to solutions?

To answer this question, we must define the difference between anger and aggression. Anger is a natural emotional response to a frustrating, upsetting situation. Aggression is a negative expression of that anger.

Randy's case exemplifies how aggression is a negative force which creates deep unhappiness in the person who wields it. He was furious when, for the fourth time in a row, his six-year-old daughter, Kim, and ten-year-old son, Brad, came for their visit dressed in ratty outfits they'd long outgrown. Each also carried a paper bag full of equally tattered clothing.

"I felt like screaming and crying at the same time when I saw the way they were dressed," Randy, a hospital technician, recalled. "Suddenly, I realized what my ex-wife, Virginia, was doing. She was purposefully sending the kids over looking like bums so that I'd buy them new clothes. I must have spent eight hundred dollars in two months just on new outfits for Kim and Brad. With the child support I pay, that's a lot of money to me!''

Instead of confronting his ex-wife with his legitimate complaint, he sat the children down and reeled off every fault he could think of about their mother. He told them about Virginia's teen-age experimentation with marijuana. About affairs she'd had at work. The names she had called the children behind their backs.

The horrified youngsters listened as their father shredded the image they held of their mother. Kim cried for him to stop, but Randy didn't stop until he had used up all his anger at Virginia. Of course, Virginia didn't suffer much as a result of this outburst, since she was not present. The rest of the weekend was unusually quiet, as the children timidly tried to put their father's behavior in perspective. They were too young, however, to see their role in Randy's quest for revenge. And, instead of taking his side as Randy had expected, Kim and Brad began to display signs of stress.

The night of Randy's outburst, Kim wet her bed for the first time since she was a toddler. That same night, Brad had the first of what was to be a recurring nighmare about being chased by a monster that wanted to eat him. Within a month of the incident, both children's schoolwork began to decline. Fortunately, an alert school counselor noticed the changes, intervened, and provided some family guidance before more serious damage occurred.

Randy didn't intend to hurt his children. But he knew of no other way—he didn't stop and consider any other way—of dealing with his anger. Some things Randy could have done will be presented at the end of this chapter.

Roger's story is similar to Randy's; he ended up hurting himself when he sought revenge against his ex-wife. Roger had divorced his first wife and lost custody of their son. When I met him, his second wife and their twin daughters had also left him. He described himself as a ''super failure. I didn't think I could do anything right.''

But as so often happens, his self-blame turned into anger at his ex-spouse. ''I began thinking about how she had left me. It was really sneaky, because she had waited until I was gone, looking for work in California, and then she moved! I found out about it when I got the divorce papers in the mail.'' Roger shook his head and pretended to scratch an itch as he wiped away a tear.

In his fury, Roger wrote his second wife a series of abusive letters in which he graphically described what he wanted to do to her to teach her a lesson. "I don't know why I thought writing her was going change things," he said in his raspy cigarette-smoker voice, shutting his eyes tightly. "Looking back, I can't account for much of my actions right then. I was in a fog for the longest time, and I didn't even know how messed up I was until Rita got restraining orders against me seeing her and the girls. It was on account of those letters."

Again, at the time Roger's actions felt perfectly justifiable. He had a right to be angry. He felt his wife had wronged him and seemed to see no other way to redress the situation.

Closely related to aggression is passive-aggression. As opposed to screaming and bullying aggressive behavior, passive-aggressive behavior is a less combative, indirect means to communicate anger. It is common among people who have difficulty saying no. The passive-aggressive person will respond, "Yes, I will do that," but end up saying "No, I won't" with his or her behavior.

For example, Pat had agreed, after surrendering custody of her seven-year-old son, to pay two hundred dollars a month child support. But she greatly resented having to do so; she believed it was a "man's job" to support the family. So, she'd often "forget" to send the child support check or make it out for the wrong amount "by accident." Pat may or may not have been conscious of these mistakes when she made them. They were an indirect expression of anger that she could have worked out by discussing her feelings with her ex-husband, taking legal steps to change her child support order, or by consulting a mental health professional about how to accept the situation or by learning how to express her anger directly and appropriately.

Darren also expressed his anger over losing custody of his son and daughter in a passive-aggressive manner. To the vexation of his frantic ex-wife, he consistently returned the children from visitations several hours after the agreed-upon time. "Telling the old lady about how I feel won't do any good," he insisted. Darren was partly right. Discussing his anger with his ex-wife wouldn't have resulted in a change in custody. But it would have helped him lessen his discomfort, and open a channel of communication with his ex-wife, based on honesty rather than undermining one another. Such discussions could eventually lead to increasing Darren's visitation periods with the children.

Another common and unhealthy passive-aggressive pattern is to try to show up one's ex-spouse by becoming a "Disneyland Mommy" or "Disneyland Daddy." That is what Peggy did to get back at her ex-husband for what she considered the brutal way in which he took custody from her.

During each visitation, Peggy, a thirty-three-year-old executive with least access, took her two pre-teen sons to an amusement park, movie, or arcade, followed by a toy store shopping spree. It wasn't long before the children stopped appreciating how Peggy showered them with gifts, and instead, started expecting it. In trying to make her ex-husband sorry for what he did, she was creating some very undesirable attitudes in her sons.

All these episodes of aggressive and passive-aggressive behavior have one theme in common: *futility*. The angry behavior accomplished nothing positive. You do need to release your anger, but using aggression to do this sends you backwards; it erodes your self-esteem and your relationships with other people—people whose cooperation you need. There are ways to draw on your anger that get you what you want, or bring you as close as possible to getting what you want.

The Assertive Parent

Perhaps more than you ever have before, during your custody crisis you need to hone your assertiveness skills. Assertive behavior is a direct way of communicating anger that produces positive results for both parents and children. It is a nonmanipulative means of searching for and negotiating favorable results while still acknowledging the feelings of anger. There are ways to communicate these feelings without the bulldozing effects of aggression or the fruitless conspiracies of passive-aggression.

Frank provides a good example of assertive behavior. Soon after separating from his wife, Frank noticed his children Ginny and Stan becoming increasingly unruly. The son and daughter who had always been well-mannered and polite now snapped orders at adults and ignored Frank's attempts at discipline. Frank felt trapped. He didn't want to spend his short custody visits yelling at the kids, but he also didn't want to condone Ginny and Stan's behavior.

When Frank finally met his ex-wife's boyfriend, he felt sure the children were behaving in troublesome ways because of their new home environment. He waited to calm down, then approached his ex-wife to discuss his concerns. She defensively denied that her boyfriend was the culprit behind the children's behavior problems.

Instead of spiraling into another argument, Frank waited until his next visitation and took the children to a local child psychologist. There Stan and Ginny were able to talk about their feelings surrounding the divorce. In fact, they were so relieved to have a chance to express their emotions that they requested to continue seeing the therapist. Two months later, both the children and Frank reported that therapy had helped immensely in relieving the tense situation.

To be assertive in the custody crisis, parents must stand their ground firmly and insist on upholding their rights. An assertive parent expects competent service from an attorney or calmly finds another. The assertive parent seeks equity for all concerned by being punctual with child support payments and adhering to visitation agreements. If child support or visitation agreements seem unfair, the assertive parent consults the ex-spouse. If this does not produce satisfactory results, he or she seeks legal counsel. The assertive parent doesn't step on anyone's toes, but does mean business.

Throughout all dealings, the assertive parent is aware of his or her own feelings and expresses them openly to others. But this is done without blame, and without expecting a particular response. That is, the assertive parent doesn't use emotion as a tool to manipulate. Rather, he or she channels this anger into a positive course of action saying, "This situation really makes me mad. There is more than one way to act here. What are all the things I *could* do? Which is most fair? Which will get me what I want in the long run? Which will solve this particular problem once and for all with a minimum of fuss? Which should I avoid and why? Which is best for the children?" and so forth.

For example, I found myself in the same situation Randy had been in; after paying several hundred dollars each month in child support, I felt enraged every time I saw my children dressed in worn, shabby clothing. What was even more frustrating to me was that I felt compelled during many of our visitations to make a trip to the local mall to replenish my sons' wardrobes. Over several months I spent hundreds of dollars on little boys' pants, shirts, and shoes.

Yet, every time they'd come to visit, the boys would still arrive with a suitcase full of clothes that even the Salvation Army would have rejected. My blood really boiled when I finally realized that my ex-husband was tricking me into buying the boys new clothes.

I finally resolved this situation by insisting—without harshness—that I pack my sons' clothes when I picked them up at my ex-husband's house before each visit. This way, I was able to make sure the boys arrived at my house with adequate underwear and properly-fitting clothes, as well as getting an accurate idea of exactly what clothes Chuck and Grant did need. And very importantly, I released my anger while avoiding an ugly scene with my ex-husband.

I don't mean to suggest that this kind of calm problem-solving is easy, or that once you get the knack of it, the emotional wrenches of your custody loss will disappear. Far from it. Take the case of Mary. She was unhappy that she could only have her six-year-old son Jason on the weekends. But even more troubling was her ex-husband Steve's announcement that he planned to move with the boy to another city two hundred miles away. Mary was very angry that her ex-husband was dictating when and where she'd see Jason. After stewing about the situation for three months, she decided to seek a legal block against his moving away. In case that didn't work, she had an alternative—"If I don't get the court order making Steve stay here, I'll move to the same city he goes to." It wouldn't be easy for Mary to pack up and move and find new employment, but this was the action she finally settled on as being best for her and for her son. And yet, for another parent in different circumstances, such a drastic move could turn out to be a personal disaster.

Assertiveness How-to

Since anger is inevitable during the custody crisis, the sooner you make a move to plan how to handle this anger assertively, the better. Preparing and having a plan of action for anger is like plotting an escape route in case of a fire. With some forethought about how to handle it, anger need not feel like an unwelcome stowaway. It is an inherent part of being human, its expression is more controllable than you may have thought, and it can be a catalyst for expending the energy necessary to protect your rights.

Like any new habit, assertiveness—communicating honestly without trying to dominate the conversation and without subordinating your rights and wishes—requires consistent effort to become integrated into your personality. At first, it may feel awkward to rephrase the way you speak; it may feel phony or contrived. Stick with it, however, because the results are worth it.

A big part of assertiveness training is learning to approach a subject in a way that increases the opportunity for communication and decreases the chance that the listener will become defensive. A tried and true way to do this is to use "I messages," that is, statements in which you "own" your feelings instead of blaming them on others. Compare the following aggressive and assertive remarks:

Aggressive	*Assertive*
You never let the kids talk with me on the phone! You make me so angry! (Uses sweeping terms like "never" or "always"; implies the other has deliberately done something wrong.)	*I* feel angry because I can't reach the kids when I call, even though we agreed which days and times I should call. Let's both stick to the schedule we set up. (Directly states feelings and wishes; suggests a solution.)
You better let me see the kids over Christmas vacation or I'll call my lawyer tomorrow! (Puts problem entirely onto the other person; makes threats.)	I'd like to arrange the days I can have the kids during the holidays. Let's try to work something out peacefully. (States wishes and protects rights, but shows willingness to compromise to reach a solution.)
You really screwed up when you told Johnnie he could get his driver's license! Boy, you're as stupid as ever! (Blames, insults, and humiliates the other person.)	I'm pretty upset that you promised Johnnie his driver's license. Let me tell you why I think he's too young . . . (Expresses feelings without blame; gives reasons for concerns; invites analysis of the problem.)

Sometimes "I messages" are really "You messages" in disguise: "I think you're an imbecile!"

You probably have the idea by now. The content of the message, the intent behind the statement and the way the statement is delivered all determine whether it's aggressive or assertive! "You messages" tend to make the listener think more about how to defend him- or herself than about what it is you're saying. So, even if you're fuming at the other person, it's to your advantage to take a few minutes to cool off before speaking your piece. If, in the middle of an interaction, you feel your blood beginning to boil, know it is not the time to act or speak. Say something to unhook from the situation and buy time, like "I need to think about that and get back to you." And when you do speak, if in doubt about what to say, just relay your "here and now" feelings in an honest and direct manner. Stay aware of your facial expressions, body language, and tone of voice; they make a big difference. At least seventy percent of your message—how you come across—is nonverbal.

I have to add that honest and direct communication can be abused in a couple of ways. First, some people use honesty as an excuse to blurt out their frank opinions. They'll insult you and then argue that they were just being honest with you. Remember that assertive people always try to respect the feelings and rights of others. This includes respect for your own feelings and rights, which brings me to the second way assertiveness is commonly abused. When you lay open your feelings to others in inappropriate situations, you leave yourself vulnerable to being hurt. While I'm a strong believer in the need for rigorous honesty, I also feel that a part of taking care of yourself is knowing when to keep quiet. There are some people with whom I choose not to share my feelings for some of the following reasons: they don't have my best interests in mind and may want to know how I feel in order to use it against me; they're intoxicated or in a completely different frame of mind from mine; the setting we're in is inappropriate for a frank discussion; we don't have enough time to open and close a touchy issue.

Just as you appreciate knowing where you stand with others, so will they appreciate it from you. You'll really be teaching people how to treat you—like an intelligent, mature adult, not like a punching bag or a doormat. Lastly, practicing assertion reduces self-defeating episodes of lashing out in anger, because you deal with anger effectively when it arises, rather than letting it build up over time.

Handling Anger Nondestructively

Assertiveness is a primary instrument for the person experiencing anger in the custody crisis. Another way to reduce anger—especially when it feels absolutely overwhelming—is to diligently search for something positive in every situation. The great thing about anger and blame is—they're easy. It's much harder to maintain a sense of perspective and admit that you made some mistakes, the other person made some mistakes, and that there are some negatives and some positives. If you have no patience for finding the bright side of a situation, or find the idea of soul-searching when you're hopping mad ridiculous, your anger still needs to be dealt with, not ignored or masked.

The best way to relieve hostility is through letting go. This process involves physical activity such as crying and shouting, or hitting an inanimate object. The key to letting go is to make sure the activity is viewed strictly as a way to let off steam. If, for example, you hit a pillow with the intention of releasing anger, it will be effective for you. You will feel drained, but relieved. But if the pillow-hitting is accompanied by a mental image of actually striking your ex-spouse or lawyer, you can expect to get angrier. The same is true of shouting. You shouldn't shout *at* someone, rather, shout *out* your feelings of anger and helplessness. You may want to do this in the presence of a close friend or therapist for support. Remember, it is never appropriate to do these letting go exercises in front of young children. Adolescents, however, may benefit from joining in this exercise with you—it can turn a tense time together into a warm and even fun one.

If you have never released anger in this way, you probably feel self-conscious just thinking about doing it. Women in particular have been encouraged from childhood that to completely let go, to scream and shout, is improper or a sign of instability. Paradoxically though, letting go increases your stability and centeredness; it puts you in control of when and where you deal with your anger. Since we all get angry, we all need to let go occasionally.

In addition, there's nothing like vigorous exercise to release anger. If you've never tried this method, you don't know what you're missing! I seriously recommend twenty minutes of aerobic exercise—walking, running, swimming, or biking—three or four times a week to help you cope with your anger in a positive way (not to mention generally feeling better).

Keep practicing the feeling awareness exercises we discussed in the last chapter.

Another proven method for replacing internal turmoil with quiet serenity is the use of positive affirmations. These statements are spoken either silently or out loud to oneself at least twice a day. Some therapists suggest writing down the affirmations, as well as saying them, explaining that the act of writing further integrates the thoughts into our consciousness. My own preference is to tape-record affirmations and then play the tape every morning when I'm fixing my hair and putting on my make-up. Listening to these positive messages, spoken in my own voice, gives me an upbeat feeling for the rest of the day.

Some suggested affirmations appear below. But you are encouraged to *create additional statements that have personal meaning for you and your situation.* Update them as time goes on and keep them posted where you can see them:

—I know that I am a good parent and have done everything possible for my children.

—I play a powerful role in my children's lives and exert a positive influence on them in every way.

—My children know that I love them, and I know that they love me.

—My children will be able to understand and accept what happened when they get older and have more experience. Until that time, I will try my best to protect them from suffering from any bitterness between my ex-spouse and me.

—I did everything possible to have custody of my children.

—I am a good person in every way, no matter where my children live.

—By paying child support, I remind myself and my children that I care a great deal about them.

—It's okay for me to be happy, with or without my children.

—I take care of myself by expressing my anger directly and assertively.

—I uphold all my rights and am considerate of the rights of others.

—Today I will focus on accepting the things I cannot change and take steps to change the things I can.

—I take responsibility for my life, my feelings, and my happiness.

—I can take care of myself in any situation that comes up and I trust myself to know what to do.

—I have the right to feel angry. My feelings are always justified and legitimate because they belong to me.

—I have the right to express my anger. To the best of my ability, I will express it in a nondestructive, positive manner.

4

"I'm Losing Control"
The Panic Stage

*I can't stand the fact that my ex can tell me
when and where I get to see my kids! It feels
like I have absolutely no say-so in their lives at
all, and you know, I really think it's just a big
power trip to my ex, because all she's interested in is dangling the kids in front of me and
controlling me with that.*
— Father, two years after losing
custody of his three children

Wayne had methodically planned most of his life. He knew what
college he would attend. What bank he would work for after
graduation. Even the position he would eventually hold—bank
president. He successfully wooed the woman of his dreams—
Amanda, the tall blonde insurance saleswoman who became his wife
and the mother of his daughter and two sons. At forty-one, Wayne
felt securely in control of his life and his destiny.

But there was one event Wayne hadn't foreseen. After seven
years of marriage, Amanda suddenly asked for a divorce, demanding
custody of the children, the house, his BMW, and a substantial
amount of money in child support. After recovering from the initial
shock of the divorce and the absence of his children, Wayne found
that for once, it seemed he had lost control over his life. How could
he have been so blind to Amanda's dissatisfaction?

His self-confidence shaken, he began to wonder what else he
could be blind to. How thoroughly had he reviewed the big loan he
approved last week? How loyal were his employees? If Amanda

could leave him, could his staff be secretly planning to depart as well?

Many of us, thrust into the custody crisis, can identify with Wayne. We may feel that we were once able to count on tomorrow being pretty much like today. Now, we cannot anticipate, or are afraid to anticipate, what will happen from one day to the next. There is the horrible realization, "I'm not calling the shots here at all!"

In terms of the progression of the grief stages, panic, defined as "sudden, overwhelming terror," often first appears at the point at which we become painfully, consciously aware that custody will definitely be lost or reduced. Now desperate, we try to plan, plot, fix, and conspire to regain control. This is not surprising, considering all of the things a divorced parent seems to lose control of. And, all of the following are true for both most- and least-access parents.

First, we feel, any time the children are away from us, that we have no control over how the children are raised and whether they'll be well cared for. I, for instance, used to worry that my sons would run out in the street and be hit by a car. My fear was based on a close call Chuck had before the divorce. Another one of my nagging concerns was that my sons wouldn't dress warmly enough. I'd picture them going sleeveless in the winter and not wearing socks on cold nights. This fear was sparked by my sons' preference for dressing lightly. Like other divorced parents, I found it hard to trust my ex-spouse's judgment in matters of childcare.

Not having full custody of our children intensifies horribly the anguish of parenthood—an anguish that Judith Viorst so pointedly describes in *Necessary Losses*:

> But we also must understand that, though we might rather feel guilty than helpless, there are limits to the power parents possess. We must also understand that in both their outside world and the world inside their head, there are dangers in the lives of these children we desperately—so desperately—long to protect over which we may have no control.

Toni said she began to worry about her children's safety when a co-worker tried to comfort her. "I was told, 'Worse things could have happened than your losing custody—at least the kids are still alive and in good health.' " This well-intentioned statement caused Toni to ponder just how much worse it could have been. She began to fret that the girls would fall victim to every catastrophe imaginable—that they'd be run over by a car, that they'd fall out of their second-story window, that they'd eat contaminated food. Her intense feelings of powerlessness over her children's safety made her life a waking nightmare.

Another substantial loss is loss of control over our finances. Earlier we discussed the financial drain of custody proceedings— lawyers' fees, court-appointed psychologists' fees, the costs of evaluations and investigations, plus child support payments, travel costs for visitations, and so forth. This is a big concern for most-access parents, as well. Being the sole caregiver to a child, especially if your ex-spouse is not forthcoming with child support, can be an overwhelming financial responsibility.

It is neither shallow nor selfish to attach importance to finances. Whether we like it or not, part of our identity is tied to income, savings account balances, and material possessions. When our finances become out of control because of matters which are not in our hands, the result is a sense that *we* have lost control.

Our powerlessness is also intensified by the unexpected complexity of custody proceedings. Bombarded and intimidated by legal terms and procedures, we may have no choice but to depend on an attorney—whom we may not trust completely—to lead us through the judicial maze.

But perhaps the most frightening thing for us to lose control over during the custody crisis is our emotions. The sight of an empty baby stroller may trigger an unexpected crying spell. An innocent question about the children may provoke an angry tirade. The postponement of a visitation by a few hours can send us into a tailspin of desperate gloom.

Seemingly, fate, God, or whatever our conception of the force that drives the universe, is against us.

Bargaining and Blaming

Desperate attempts to regain the control we feel we've lost often take the form of bargaining. Like the terminally ill patient who barters with God, promising to be good if he can only live until Christmas, noncustodial parents bargain with God, with ex-spouses, with attorneys, and with themselves; in return for being good, they wish to regain full custody. "I promise to stop drinking" and "no more affairs ever" are the kinds of deals they try to strike for just one more chance at getting the kids. Dr. Kubler-Ross notes in *On Death and Dying* that bargaining behavior is grounded on the person's knowing, "from past experiences, that there is a slim chance that he may be rewarded for good behavior and be granted a wish."

This acknowledgment of loss of control is not the same thing as acceptance. In fact, since these bargains are frequently unrealistic, they can backfire disastrously. Jim, a university professor, was thrown out of the house by his wife when she discovered that he was having an affair with one of his students. He spent the next two months in an angry frenzy, trying to stop the legal procedures of divorce, trying to reason with his wife that the affair with the student had been the only infidelity and it would never happen again. He told me that finally, exhausted and crying bitterly, he got down on his knees and pleaded with God not to take his children away, promising never to cheat on his wife again, and to go to church every Sunday. But she did divorce him and gained custody of their son and daughter. He swore to God, "You didn't live up to your end of the bargain, and neither will I!" Soon after, Jim had another relationship with a young student. Word of this reached the university administration, and he was fired.

Fortunately, when most of us try to wheel and deal with God, or whomever, the results are not usually so traumatic. This behavior is very natural; we can't help trying absolutely everything we can think of to keep our kids with us. It is only when we become convinced that some last ditch effort is our only remaining chance for happiness that we risk getting hurt, like Jim did.

When we try to control everything around us, it's because, on the inside, we feel incapable of controlling anything. So, we need to start focusing on ourselves—on what we realistically can accomplish and the areas we need to work on. This is a foreign attitude to people who were raised to always be self-sacrificing and never selfish. But, if you spend some time thinking about you, understanding you, taking better care of you, you will feel more in control. When we focus only on others, we come to expect them to fulfill us and make us happy. We try to make them responsible for what goes on in our lives and how we feel. And this is where blaming begins.

Blame comes into the picture once again, simply because if you can put your finger on who or what caused your loss, you seem to regain a sense of control over your life. So, we may indict others or the world in general for our custody loss, completely absolving ourselves. It's usually a lot easier to blame directly some actual person or entity—God, a lawyer, an ex-spouse—than it is to blame an abstract social system or some complex set of circumstances that happened over a long period of time. Assigning blame, though, is a temporary comfort. First, you probably don't really believe it—deep down, you know or suspect you had something to do with your custody situation. This leads to inner conflict and turmoil in the same way that repressing your feelings or being dishonest with yourself does. Furthermore, if you lay total blame on someone or something outside yourself, it means you had *no control* over what happened. You are the helpless victim of an unjust world. If you continue to believe this, you may become tense and overly cautious, concluding that you must always be on guard, and that "it's better to be safe than sorry." In addition, you may believe that you are powerless over your own future. You have no power to mold your own destiny; you are paralyzed, focusing all your energy on warding off potential perils.

Or, some of us may turn around and blame ourselves completely. This belief also comes with a hefty price tag, because if you have given yourself all the control over what happened, you again paralyze yourself, this time with self-loathing and isolating guilt. You messed it all up, so now you, alone, god-like, must somehow pick up the pieces and put it all back together.

Living in Fear

Irrational fears can grow out of our sense that the world is a harsh, unpredictable place that has wrenched our children away. We may develop these fears in areas of our lives other than parenting, such as work or school, as a way of generalizing or "spreading around" the anxieties generated by not having our children with us. As Stanley Keleman writes in *Living Your Dying*:

> Each of us is afraid to express anger and sadness, afraid to cry and mourn the loss of part of ourselves that we have had to surrender at different stages of our lives. Each of us is afraid to lose control of ourselves in this way. But when grief cannot be properly expressed, it will emerge as part of our unlived lives—our fantasies and fears.

Parental fears often take the form of a feeling of impending doom. In addition to worrying that something horrible will happen to the children when they're away from us, we fear the airplane or car we are riding in is about to crash, that the house will be burgled or it will burn down, that once people know we have lost custody, we will be shunned because we are "bad luck." Anything that seems out of our control can become the focus for fear. Karl, for instance, became absolutely convinced that, because he had lost custody of his son, he was also going to be fired from his job. (But he was overjoyed when, instead of handing him a pink slip, Karl's boss called him into his office and gave him a raise and a promotion!)

Sarah enrolled in college after her children went to live with their father. She dreamed of one day becoming a psychotherapist and helping others, but she repeatedly struggled with fears that she was spinning her wheels and getting nowhere. "I know that all this schooling will eventually get me a degree," she told me, "but sometimes it feels like I'm doing something wrong and that someone's going to tell me that I can't be a therapist. It feels like I'll go to classes for years and years and at the end of it all, someone will tell me I'm not good enough to be a therapist." Sarah's self-esteem and her sense of control over her future were both shaky after her custody loss. She worked on herself in therapy—enumerating and appreciating her many abilities, including her ability to handle any as yet unforeseen problems. She slowly regained her confidence and sense of personal competence. I think Sarah's going to make a great therapist someday.

Another noncustodial mother named Laura told me that she feared other mothers wouldn't want her to be around their children. This stemmed from Laura's painful awareness that others must think she was an unfit mother to have lost custody. "I can't help but wonder what they think about my abilities to take care of children," Laura reflected, "especially since none of my friends have asked me to baby-sit for them since my custody loss. I'm afraid to ask them why . . . I'm afraid of what I might hear."

Some parents' fears take the form of recurrent nightmares of their children suffering or of reliving the courtroom trial.

"It got to where I was afraid to fall asleep," Daniel, a thirty-year-old noncustodial father of two recalled with a shudder. "I kept having these dreams where my ex-wife would be driving this huge rig—an eight-wheeler truck—and she'd have the kids with her in the cab of the truck. They'd be laughing and having a good time, but all the while they're driving straight towards me. I have to run my tail off to keep her from driving over me and then half-way through the dream—right before I wake up—I suddenly can't run at all. It's like I'm going in slow motion."

To sum up, when something's been lost to us, we tend to retain a residual sense of insecurity and personal danger; we behave as though we're tip-toeing through a mine field, waiting for the next disaster to strike. It can be hard to distinguish whether these fears are coming from real or imagined sources. In the next section, we'll look at ways to ease this fearfulness.

Regaining Confidence

Aside from the healing passage of time, there are things we can do to alleviate fears and increase our sense of self-confidence. One immediate thing that can be done is to practice relaxation techniques to calm fears and reduce stress; these include relaxation cassette tapes, meditation, and exercise.

Fears keep us from trying new things. We often wait for the "perfect" moment or conditions to arise before undertaking something new. Such procrastination can all too easily become a lifetime habit of waiting for a safer, better climate in which to undertake our goals and dreams.

Anna had always dreamed of being a professional singer. Up until the time of her custody loss, she had always reasoned that she needed to be at home with her children, not off somewhere at a singing engagement. After her husband won custody of their son and daughter in an emotionally and financially draining custody battle, Anna had the time available to pursue her dream. That's when she froze.

"I feel so stuck," Anna complained. "I want to go to a singing coach, but I'm so scared!" We looked at the different fears Anna was experiencing and found that among her fears of success and failure, she was also suffering from the "imposter phenomenon." In other words, Anna felt like a fake everytime she thought about singing in front of an audience. This is not an unusual occurrence among people with high goals and aspirations. Successful people, in particular, often believe they don't deserve the recognition they've received. They fear that they'll be exposed for the fakes they are, and then all the trappings of success will be revoked. Anna felt that people who were successful singers were somehow genetically different than other people. She remarked that she felt as if the singers she admired had always been famous.

Today, Anna is enthusiastically pursuing her singing career. What happened? Anna finally accepted the fact that she had to take action before she could overcome her fears and insecurities. This meant enrolling in singing classes and auditioning before coaches and audiences, regardless of how scared she was. This is true for almost any fear you want to overcome—first you take action, then you gain confidence in your abilities—not vice versa.

What is your secret dream or desire? What would you like to accomplish this month, this year? Is there an occupation, hobby or something you've always wanted to try, but some nagging fear holds you back? Do you fear:

—that you will fail? There's no such thing as a failure, just someone who stops trying too soon. If you want something worthwhile and you consistently put your best effort forward, the majority of your attempts will result in success. But, perhaps even more importantly, when you do not accomplish what you wanted to, invariably you will find that you learned something useful in the attempt—something which can help you later on.

—that you will succeed? Success often brings radical change and change means S-T-R-E-S-S. Increased responsibility is frightening ("Can I handle it?") and an increased income creates unexpected stress in the form of "Now I can't use the excuse of not having the money."

In my practice I've found that a tremendous amount of healing occurs when people give themselves permission to acquire new skills. They feel re-energized and more alive because they are learning again. They meet new people. Learn new things about themselves. And they regain that childlike enthusiasm and curiosity so vital to happiness.

Here are some steps that may help you get started:

1. Write down what you want to accomplish—anything and everything from "speak to my ex-spouse about the children's

schedule" to your wildest dreams. You don't need to show it to anyone—not yet.

2. Close your eyes and imagine yourself realizing this goal, including as many details in your mental image as you can. Afterward, ask yourself what feelings accompanied this image. Excitement? Disbelief? Fear? Contentment?

3. Allow yourself to experience these feelings, and if fear was a predominant emotion, think about some of the reasons why you experienced it. Allow fear to live in you, but don't let it stop you from taking the next step.

4. Next, write down one or two small steps you could take *today* in order to bring one of your goals closer to reality. This could include making a telephone call or ordering a booklet. It may also involve picking the brains of people who have already accomplished your goal. Or it may mean a trip to the library. There's always something you can do RIGHT NOW toward fulfilling your dreams and goals.

5. Do one small step.

6. Repeat steps 4 and 5 tomorrow.

I've seen people completely turn around their lives by adopting this method of approaching problems they thought could never be solved. One dramatic example was Bobbie, an attractive thirty-three-year-old woman who almost had to be hospitalized for suicidal impulses. When I first met Bobbie, she spoke of continual crying spells and of having a hopeless attitude toward life. Her condition came about following the loss of custody of her six-year-old daughter to her ex-husband. After her daughter moved out, Bobbie felt she had no reason for living. She began acting very self-destructively by overeating and abusing alcohol.

After several months of therapy, Bobbie had progressed to the point where she had stopped abusing her body. But lack of meaning in her life still confronted her daily. "I just hate to get up in the morning to go to work," she'd complain during every session. We looked into Bobbie's job, and found that she had drifted into—rather than chosen—her occupation of secretary. What she really wanted to do was work that involved her long-time hobby of gardening.

Our next few sessions centered around Bobbie taking the steps named above. She first contacted the Small Business Administration to find out about loans to start a nursery. Then she enrolled in night school. While taking classes in business and horticulture, Bobbie continued taking action by getting to know people in related businesses. She interviewed gardeners, landscapers, peatmoss sales-people, you name it. And to watch her now, you would never guess that at one time Bobbie was too scared to even admit the dream to herself. Now her enthusiasm spurs her on and she estimates she'll be opening shop in about a year.

When you break it down into small steps, the world is much more manageable. And as you manage your life the way you want to, your self-confidence returns.

Taking Responsibility for the Past

Our goal, in healing from custody loss, is to attain a sense of *balance* in assessing who is responsible. This is the way to regain a true sense of control over your past. You will probably identify several things you could have done differently, or perhaps one thing—"This is where I went wrong." In doing this, you actually give yourself power; you did have the power to influence certain things, but perhaps you either did not use that power or, you used it negatively. Perhaps there are changes you can make to turn these things to your favor in the future. Renee, for example, lost custody of her three-year-old son, Joey, largely because her ten-hour workdays meant he would have to spend most of the day in a nursery. Her ex-husband was considered the parent better able to care for Joey because his new wife could stay home with the boy all day. Renee could not alter the fact that she needed to work to support herself, but she realized she was partially responsible because of her very long workday. She resolved to continue fighting for custody and cut back to an eight-hour day if she got Joey back.

Be sure to keep your self-assessment on the level of "responsi-bility" instead of "blame" or "fault." The latter two terms tend to push all our childhood buttons of feeling helpless, weak, resentful, that life's unfair, etc. Responsibility, on the other hand, implies maturity and the hope that you, as an intelligent adult, may be able to take action to resolve the problems involved. This is an active stance, whereas someone who says, "It was all my fault. I'm to blame" often has a depressive, what's-the-use-anyway attitude.

Ask yourself what parts of the custody situation you were, or are, responsible for. Some of these may include:

—The details of how and why the divorce was initiated. Be sure to examine all the pressures and problems that led up to it, not just the incident that broke the camel's back.

—Your actions during the marital separation. You made some life-changing decisions as the marriage was ending—many of them made under extreme duress. Nonetheless, these actions and decisions likely played a large role in determining your current life situation.

—Your choice of attorney. How did you pick your attorney? A friend's recommendation? Out of the yellow pages? How many did you interview before deciding, and what criteria did you use in arriving at your decision? While choosing an attorney is a little like shopping with a blindfold on, there are certain self-protective measures we can take in making this important decision. For instance, we can talk to others who have gone through a custody battle, or spend a day in the courtroom audience to see the different styles of attorneys.

—Reasons you lost or gave up custody or reasons for the current arrangement. What reasons were stated by the judge or mediator? In what ways were these fair? Unfair? What were your life circumstances then and how are they different now? What steps are you taking or will you take starting today, a little bit each day, to improve a negative situation or negative feelings about yourself that helped lead to your custody situation?

You may ask, "What's the use of such an exercise? I can't change what happened." Although it's true that you can't reach back into the past and change your actions, you can face and accept your own mistakes. You can recognize that those mistakes do not diminish your worth as a person. You can enumerate and put to use all the things you've learned from your wrong moves. And you can forgive yourself. These are the only things that any of us can do, but none of them is easy.

The Question of Control

As to the future, as your custody crisis is ongoing, the crux of the issue of control is recognizing that *there are things you can control and things you can't.* When you allow yourself to believe and accept this, you no longer carry the burden of feeling responsible for everything and everybody. If you can't control others, then you needn't expend much of your energy worrying about them.

This leaves you free to focus on things that you *can* control. For example, you may not be able to control what your ex-spouse says about you in court, but you can control what's said in your defense. Similarly, you may not be able to control the fact that you're ordered to pay child support each month, but there are legal steps you can take to lower the payment amount if it really is out of line. In addition, you may not be able to control much of your child's life when he or she isn't with you, but you can contribute what you can, such as health insurance or your expertise in algebra or English. You can identify and implement ways to keep the lines of communication open, and create an atmosphere in which, when your child does need help, he or she will want to turn to you for guidance. I, for example, learned to calm my anxiety over my sons running into the street and being hit by a car by taking the time during visitations to review with them the dangers of playing around cars. I eased my worries about whether the boys dressed warmly enough by buying them warm clothes and confirming while talking to them over the phone that they were wearing them.

When you stop trying to control others, they'll usually cooperate with you more readily. Your attorney will be more willing to return your phone calls if you don't badger him or her. Your ex-spouse will be more compliant about having the children ready on time for visitations if you're not constantly threatening him or her about having the kids ready when you arrive "or else."

A useful tool for learning to let go of futile attempts at being in control is the Serenity Prayer. Though some may balk at this seemingly sentimental and religious prose because of its connection to Alcoholics Anonymous, I have found that the prayer's sentiment has been tremendously valuable.

I first adopted the spirit of the Serenity Prayer seven months after my sons and I had separated. My psychology professor recommended it as a tool for reducing stress after reading my "stress diary"—a class assignment of keeping a daily record of tension-producing situations and our reactions to them. He could see that a great deal of my tension came from trying to control things beyond my grasp. When my stress worsened, I experimented with my professor's advice and tried the Serenity Prayer:

> God,
> Grant me the serenity
> to accept the things I cannot change,
> Courage
> to change the things I can, and
> Wisdom
> to know the difference.

When I first adopted the philosophy contained in this prayer, I was frightened. I felt like I did the first time I was faced with riding a bike without training wheels. Just as I couldn't imagine staying upright without those two extra wheels, I couldn't imagine letting go of any control—I was certain everything would fall apart. After all, I unconsciously believed, no one was as smart or as capable as I of knowing just how things should go or how people should act.

It took practice and patience, but over the next three or four months, I was gradually able to stop fretting about things I couldn't control. And just as I found I could ride my bike farther and faster without those extra wheels, I found that life was less frustrating and far more manageable once I decided to stop trying to control everything.

It is undeniably difficult to wrestle with the question of what you can and cannot control, especially when you're in the middle of an emotionally charged situation. Some find out through trial and error, others through stopping each time to analyze the likelihood of being able to change a situation. In each case, we should keep these priorities: being good to ourselves and others, and seeking the best for our children. It's a daily balancing act.

The examples below illustrate how this process can work.

Situation No. 1: Your ex-spouse tells you he or she is taking you to court for more child support money.

What you can't control: Your ex-spouse's behavior; your ex-spouse's lawyer's behavior.

What you CAN control: Choosing the best attorney you can; doing research on current laws; knowing what your rights are; being prompt in returning all paperwork to your attorney; appearing in court on your assigned date.

Situation No. 2: Your ex-spouse calls you and cries on your shoulder about how inconvenient this weekend's visitation with the kids will be for him or her, and asks if you can please wait another week, month, etc., to see the children.

What you can't control: Your ex-spouse's feelings or behavior. You're not responsible for either one and it's not up to you to rescue him or her.

What you CAN control: Choosing whether or not you wish to go along with the request. Make sure it's YOUR CHOICE.

Situation No. 3: The children tell you that your ex-spouse is saying demeaning things about you and calling you vicious names to their faces.

What you can't control: Your ex-spouse's angry, vindictive feelings about you.

What you CAN control: Talking to your ex-spouse about the allegation. If it is true, take immediate legal steps to get a "no disparaging remarks" clause put into your custody paperwork (one phone call to your attorney should be enough to accomplish this). Let your ex-spouse know about the clause, and stress that it will be followed up if violated. Furthermore, you can discuss with your children the ways people act when they're angry and hurt. This will help them keep the disparaging remarks in perspective. (Don't let this degenerate into a name-calling session on your part!)

Situation No. 4: Your child acts awkwardly when he or she first sees you after spending time with the other parent.

What you can't control: The normal behavior of your child. Children normally feel dazed, anxious or depressed right after switching from one parent to the other. Remember, as much as you love your child, you really cannot—nor should you try to—rescue him or her from emotional pain. If you try, your child may cover up or stuff feelings in an attempt to please you.

What you CAN control: You can lessen the impact, but probably not eliminate it, by sticking to a set routine for the pick-ups and drop-offs of visitations—always at the same time on the same day at the same location. And you can help your children verbalize their feelings and accept the validity of their feelings. If your daughter says, "I hate leaving Daddy," your response can be nonjudgmental and validating: "I know you love Daddy and it must hurt." (See chapter 7 for more on talking to children about their feelings.)

Situation No. 5: Someone makes an ignorant, insulting or vicious remark about your custody status.

What you can't control: The general attitudes people hold regarding custodial and noncustodial men and women.

What you CAN control: Taking the opportunity to educate people who are ignorant of the facts regarding custody issues; choosing to forget the person's remarks (be careful not to repress feelings, however), chalking it up to their ignorance.

Situation No. 6: Your child wants to play on a soccer team, but because of every-other-weekend visits, would not be able to attend Saturday afternoon practices and games regularly.

What you can't control: Your child's feelings of disappointment.

What you CAN control: Request that your ex-spouse cooperate in taking the child to practices and games; help to form a team that meets every other weekend for other kids in this situation. (There are millions who share the same problem.)

Situation No. 7: Your ex-spouse constantly threatens to take you back to custody court unless you comply with his or her wishes and demands.

What you can't control: Your ex-spouse's feelings of vindictiveness, anger, insecurity, or need to control, abuse, or dominate.

What you CAN control: Your behaviorial reactions to his or her threats. They are used to bully you into submission and are a form of harrassment. (It's important not to buy into them, thereby reinforcing them.) Contact your lawyer if necessary; this form of emotional blackmail is abusive and illegal.

Try asking yourself what you can and can't control. Try, just for today, not to control anyone else's behavior and see what happens. Some people, accustomed to your controlling ways, may express surprise. You'll probably notice a reduction in tension after just one day's experiment. And, if you're like most, the results will be so positive that you'll begin to look for ways to resist going back to your old, controlling ways.

This is what happened to Derek. He was so sure that his ex-wife, Terri, would forget some vital element of their daughters' care if he didn't remind her, he developed the habit of criticizing her every time he picked up the girls for a visitation. He felt Terri wouldn't see the "right" things to do unless he continually pointed them out to her. Not surprisingly, visits began and ended on a tense, often hostile note between Derek and Terri. It wasn't until his teen-age daughter complained that Derek was "always on Mom's back about something" that he noticed how controlling he'd become.

On the next visit, Derek consciously made an effort to keep the peace, and he even complimented Terri on how nice the house looked. Terri's mouth dropped open with shock, but her daughter beamed a bright smile. That week marked the beginning of some very pleasant weekends for Derek and his two daughters. And, Terri's parenting skills didn't go down the tubes after Derek stopped trying to control her. On the contrary, the girls seemed happier than ever, and Derek found it was more and more possible to believe in his ex-wife's own common sense.

What we all need at this stage is some faith—faith in ourselves, our ex-spouses, and our children, and faith in a spiritual power greater than ourselves. Indeed, it can be very difficult to maintain our self-confidence and centeredness while ignoring the spiritual dimension of our lives. But each person's exploration of this dimension is different in form and meaning. This is a good time to do some thinking about your own personal experience of faith. Perhaps for you, faith means trust in God. If you do not believe in any spiritual being, think about the last time you felt free and joyful, living only for that moment, trusting that you belonged in the world. Have faith that you can and will recapture that serenity, that you can reflect on it whenever you need to. Faith will help you to reclaim a realistic sense of your own power to make your world a safe and pleasant place.

5

Sadness, Tears, and Despair

*I feel like I'm living in a black, swirling abyss.
I know that I don't like today, but I'm also
not really looking forward to tomorrow. The
only reason I keep going is stubbornness. Most
of my energy is spent trying not to let other
people see the pain I'm in.*
—Parent without custody
for six months

Virtually every parent coping with separation from his or her children experiences depression—that bleak, immobile state in which every movement, every thought takes excruciating effort. When depression settles in, it seems as though the desolation, tears, and lethargy will never end. The world looks drab and colorless. Nothing seems humorous.

Most of us will feel some signs of depression—low energy levels, ongoing sadness and a lack of interest in anything—during the first four to six months following the loss of custody. At least some symptoms of depression are to be expected as par for the course, but their intensity does vary dramatically from person to person.

Sadness is a natural reaction to losing anyone or anything that's important to us. As parents with drastically reduced access to our children, we are sad because we have lost that daily contact and we have lost our roles as traditional mothers or fathers. Our sadness is equal to the profundity of this loss. We are also faced with the unappealing task of filling up the time left empty by our children's departure.

Triggers for Tears

Some of the most sorrowful moments as a noncustodial parent center around the holidays. Christmas is especially difficult, with the sentimental greeting cards and holiday television shows about family harmony that slam home the message, over and over, "my kids don't live with me anymore." Indeed, the first Christmas parents spend alone can be the lowest point of the custody crisis. Buying presents for the children, knowing they'll be enjoyed at the ex-spouse's home, is often an unbearable effort.

Other holidays that revolve around children, such as Easter, can be hard for the same reasons. We can also expect quite a tug at the heart on our children's birthdays. "Every year on my son's birthday, I feel depressed," one parent explained. "It's all too clear on that day that I don't have custody, because if I did, I'd be at his birthday party and not sitting at home all alone."

Mother's Day and Father's Day are also annual triggers for deep feelings of grief. Many a noncustodial parent has waited all day, hoping a former spouse will remind the children to call to wish him or her a happy Father's or Mother's Day. It's with a heavy heart that parents with least access reminisce over greeting cards the children made for them in years past and wonder whether the kids will send them one this year. Some wonder if they even deserve a Mother's Day or Father's Day card, since custody loss has left them feeling like half a parent.

Others at this stage actually find that baby food and diaper advertisements lead to depression by prompting a flood of memories about happier days of cooing infants, toothless grins and baby's first steps. For the first two or three years after my own custody loss, advertisements for infant products consistently brought tears to my eyes. In fact, I consciously avoided them for several years.

Sometimes just stumbling across the baby aisle at the supermarket or the toy section in a department store can trigger depression. "The first time I went to the grocery store after losing custody of my daughter," one parent recalled, "I took one look at the toy section and burst into tears! The last time I had been to that store, I had been with my daughter and she wanted me to buy her a small toy beauty-care set. I had told her no. Oh, how I regretted saying that when I looked at the beauty set she wanted."

The sight of a child that looks like your own can also be very painful. Shirley recalled that she had been without custody for six months when she was standing in line at her bank with a friend and caught sight of a small blonde girl playing with the velvet ropes separating the lines of customers: "That girl looked exactly like my daughter. For some reason, when I saw her I felt overwhelmed by sadness and had to dash to the bathroom because I was starting to cry. My friend didn't understand what had happened at all." Some parents report that hearing a youngster's voice that sounds like that of their own child can trigger a wave of depression. Another noncustodial parent told me that the smell of cinnamon—her daughter's favorite flavor—can send her into a crying spell.

I once became depressed on seeing an ice cream shop like one I'd been to three years earlier with my boys. It hadn't been a particularly pleasant experience. Chuck had insisted on getting an extra-large strawberry sundae, then after one bite he decided it was awful. I cried remembering how I had insisted that he take "three more bites." Looking back and regretting my ill temper of that day, I was overwhelmed by how much I missed Chuck and Grant at that moment.

Something else that brought tears to my eyes, whether the boys were with me or not, was the Small World ride at Disneyland. The dancing children, lilting theme song, and the ride's focus on how precious children are would always bring about waves of pity for myself and my sons because we were apart from one another so much of the time.

Weighed Down with Guilt

Guilt, someone once said, is what you get by holding onto an ideal and at the same time, violating it. At this stage parents are depressed and guilt-ridden precisely because they have surrendered to the inevitable; they no longer deny the fact that the kids don't live with them anymore. However, this does not live up to their ideal image of what constitutes a good mother or father. They are ashamed that the family has broken up and feel responsible for the suffering of their children. They imagine that "now my child's life is ruined . . . and it's all my fault."

This type of guilt impedes the griefwork necessary for us to move on to acceptance, because it often translates into an unwillingness for us to be self-nurturing. Sue, for instance, wouldn't allow herself to go out and have fun after losing physical custody of her son and daughter. Every time she'd go to the zoo or beach, she'd obsess over her children and think about how much they'd like to look at the animals or play in the surf.

Similarly, Hank refused to spend money on himself after his wife won custody of their three children. Invariably, he'd spend whatever he had on gifts for his children, thinking, "The kids are the ones who really need something new and fun, since I'm the one responsible for their living in such a low income situation with their mother. I don't deserve to get something new for myself."

Both Sue and Hank believed, erroneously, that they did not deserve to feel good. And both believed, again erroneously, that happiness was unobtainable as long as their children weren't living with them full-time.

Guilt eats away, termite-like, at our self-esteem as we kick ourselves for one crime—real or imagined—after another. We're haunted by thoughts such as "the children will never forgive me for initiating the divorce" or "how could I have let my mother down like this? Now she'll never get to see her grandchildren." Every time we beat ourselves up like this, self-esteem drops just a bit more. It becomes just a little more difficult to look in the mirror in the morning. The recurring thought, "I'm a bad parent" starts to sound like "I'm a bad person."

So, low self-esteem and depression feed on one another in a cyclical fashion: as we feel worse about ourselves, we become more and more depressed. The depression depletes our energy and the lethargy further prevents us from doing things that could make us feel good about ourselves, for instance, writing a letter to our children or calling to see how they are. People who are deep in depression may find that they're even unable to muster the desire to do anything after awhile, and this further erodes their self-concept. It becomes difficult to break out of this cycle without some sort of fortuitous occurrence, such as the children dropping over for a surprise visit that lifts the parent's spirits.

Such a guilt cycle becomes embedded as a habit in thinking and living. If you recognize yourself in this trap, practice the exercises at the end of this chapter; you *can* stop the practice of mentally kicking yourself. Remember, guilt in itself serves no useful purpose unless you use it to better yourself or correct a situation that is bothering you. Just sinking into a mire of self-pity and defeat doesn't get you what you want and need, nor does it do your children any good.

Another Look at Depression

"I just wanted to stay in bed and hide from the rest of the world." "I was so depressed I just wanted to give up." I've heard these remarks and ones like them from many clients and friends without custody. Feelings of futility, as well as just plain tiredness, are fairly common at this stage. After the physical and emotional stresses of the court case, which may still be ongoing, and the shock, along with the recurring bouts of anger and panic most of us have lived through to get to this point, all the fight may be drained out of us. There's a "what's the use" feeling attached to daily chores. Nothing—not caffeine, shopping, sex or good food—seems to bring anything but short-term relief from the heavy sighs and sadness. Again, these feelings may be expected for weeks or months, depending on the individual.

It's important not to deny sadness or consider it wrong. I remember one father without custody who was nonplussed by his own perfectly natural emotions: "I couldn't get my little boy's sad face and eyes out of my mind. Just the thought of how sad he was made me cry all the time and it was embarassing, you know. I'd be at work trying so hard not to think of him, but I couldn't stop. Then, I'd start crying right there at work—I'd thought I'd go nuts the way I was crying all the time like that!" Crying is one of the best outlets for your feelings. Motives for trying to avoid or bury tears and sadness range from being afraid of overwhelming feelings because of prior losses, to being taught at a young age that it isn't acceptable to express emotions. Supressing grief doesn't eliminate it and in most instances exacerbates it. Long-term problems which arise from holding grief in can range from difficulties in forming and keeping friendships to compulsive behaviors like overeating, drinking and drug abuse.

So, depression is normal. Kubler-Ross recognized the necessity of depression in her work with the terminally ill: "The patient should not be encouraged to look at the sunny side of things, as this would mean he should not contemplate his impending death. It would be contraindicated to tell him not to be sad, since all of us are tremendously sad when we lose one beloved person."

However, if severe depression lingers for several months, if chronic lethargy and sadness are so overwhelming that you ignore daily necessities such as work and eating, these are signs that your depression is more than just a natural response to loss. It may be "clinical" depression requiring attention from a physician, psychologist or psychiatrist.

Clinical depression may not go away with the passage of time and, if left untreated, can result in illness, inability to function at work or home, and suicidal impulses. Signs include long-term sadness, hopelessness or irritability. These feelings are accompanied by at least four of the following behaviors for a period of at least two weeks:

—Changes in appetite.

—Changes in sleeping habits.

—Intense feelings of restlessness or lethargy.

—Decreased sexual drive.

—Loss of interest or pleasure in or inability to maintain usual activities.

—Loss of energy or feelings of fatigue.

—Feelings of worthlessness, self-reproach or extreme guilt.

—Difficulty in concentrating or making decisions.

In addition, if a depressed person has any compelling, recurrent thoughts of death or suicide or has made a suicide attempt, immediate help through a hospital emergency room, therapist, mental health clinic, or crisis hotline should be sought.

Depression can be the longest stage of the custody crisis and the most precarious. When we are deeply depressed, we need to reach out for help, but may not know how. Long, gloomy months of sorrow prompt many parents with reduced access to their children to look for a quick fix for relieving the pain and filling the emptiness.

Unhealthy Self-Remedies for Depression

After divorcing, noncustodial parents typically live alone; this results in the isolation and boredom that are perfect breeding grounds for substance abuse. If he or she stays home after work, drinking and drugs provide instant entertainment. When the parent tries to escape the isolation, he or she may go out after work to bars, nightclubs, and friends' parties that center around alcohol and drugs.

In fact, the custody crisis often marks the first time many people become involved in anything beyond social drinking or occasional drug use. Use of chemicals—especially depressants (including alcohol), sedatives (sleeping pills) and barbiturates—can exacerbate depression. Drug use can also move a parent from normal grieving into a state of clinical depression.

Before his divorce Jeff had confined his drinking to an occasional beer after work. A year after his wife and their daughter moved out, he ended up in a hospital being treated for alcoholism.

"She had left before, so I felt sure she'd come back again," Jeff, a tall, lanky, thirty-year-old journalist, said. "When the marshal handed me the divorce papers, I knew this time she was gone for good." Jeff took his boss's advice and hired an attorney who urged Jeff to fight for custody.

"My lawyer kept me really busy. He had me fill out all kinds of forms and round up letters attesting to my character strength. For a while there, I didn't have time to even think about my wife and daughter being gone and how I felt."

Jeff continued doing paperwork and research for a month, until a friend pointed out that much of the work was the lawyer's responsibility. "My friend was right! I was furious and let my attorney know about it! After that he wrote a few form letters for me. They were meaningless, just meant to appease me after I had yelled at him." The next week he fired his attorney and began looking for a replacement. "At that point we were five weeks away from the court date." Jeff rolled a pen back and forth between his thumb and index finger and clenched his jaw as he spoke. "I was frantic! I must've interviewed every lawyer in the city before I found a half-way decent one. He did the best job he could, but with the time pressure my new lawyer couldn't pull it together quick enough to get me custody of my daughter. I became really down-in-the-dumps, and very bitter and cynical about everything."

Within four months of being denied custody, Jeff was drinking a six-pack of beer every night. He had a terrible longing for his daughter's company. He missed their times of laughter, their early evening walks, their shared secrets.

"Every night when I got home, all I'd want to do was block out my pain, so I started getting drunk until I'd pass out. At first, it was just a few beers, but gradually I built up where I was drinking almost a case of beer a night."

During this time, Jeff took great pride in the fact that he had never missed a day of work. He didn't recognize that he had developed a drinking problem, because "no alcoholic could have such a great attendance record."

After three months of consuming nearly a case of beer each night, Jeff was no longer drinking because of loneliness—he was drinking because he couldn't stop. He finally admitted he needed help when one morning, he reached for a beer to stop his hands from trembling. That night he checked in at an alcoholism treatment center.

"I was really scared at first," Jeff said. "But I knew that I'd lose everything if I didn't get some help." Thirty days later, Jeff left the center looking forward to a life of sobriety. "I'll never drink again," he had told a friend when he returned to work.

Within a few weeks he felt confident enough about his sobriety to join some friends at a comedy nightclub. He accepted the invitation telling himself he'd just drink colas. An hour into the show, his friends ordered a pitcher of beer. The waitress set an empty glass in front of him. "Maybe just one," Jeff recalled thinking. Within two weeks, he was back to drinking a case of beer a day. After another two weeks he called his counselor, who talked him into checking back into the treatment facility.

In retrospect, Jeff realized that part of the reason he returned to drinking was that he'd never completely resolved his feelings about losing custody; he had never allowed himself to cry and grieve, to face the fact that he had, indeed lost something precious to him. But he has since discovered the value of living life "one day at a time." Happily, Jeff has been sober for two years and the lessons he learned about sobriety have helped him put his custody loss into perspective. "For the first time in my life, I've found peace of mind and serenity."

Abusing substances is only one of the self-destructive, ineffective ways of dealing with depression. Another is social withdrawal. After losing custody, many parents choose to isolate themselves, hoping to find solace in solitude. This may stem, as we've discussed, from the lack of trust in others and feeling of vulnerability that follow any trauma. And, time alone is necessary. It provides an opportunity to think about what has happened and make some sense out of it.

However, habitually staying away from others, not going to work, to the store, or out with friends, is counter-productive to recovery from depression. A network of supportive people is crucial in completing the grieving process.

Ted's friends said he virtually disappeared after his wife and children left him. "He stopped coming to ballgames, and he'd go home right after work every night," one of Ted's friends recalled. His co-workers tried frantically to engage Ted in their parties and games, but Ted waved them off. Eventually, they became discouraged and quit inviting Ted to join them. Ted had dropped out of his social circle and now they had dropped him.

At first, Ted had what he wanted—to be left alone. He felt none of his buddies could relate to what was happening to him and all their light-heartedness and frivolity only added to his pain. Here he was, groping with the deepest anguish and all his friends wanted to do was drink beer and tell jokes. He felt like an eighty-year-old man in the company of six-year-olds. But it had hurt a little when he realized they weren't inviting him along anymore. Deep down, he felt it was his fault that they were avoiding him; his ex-wife's assessment that he was a no-good bum seemed entirely correct.

Ted moped around for another month in a sullen, slumped-over silence. He rarely talked, even at work. His supervisor grew alarmed at the changes in his behavior and organized a confrontation which included Ted's friends. One by one, the group told Ted that they were concerned and thought he should see a counselor.

Ted was stunned, then furious. But after he calmed down he realized his friends still cared about him: "I thought they had rejected me, just like I had done to them." With guidance therapy, Ted began trusting people. He slowly reintegrated into his network of friends and they gave him the support that eventually helped him feel good about himself again.

Others may remain physically around their friends, but be emotionally distant. They will talk about anything except their own feelings. Such people can be in a room filled with folks who care and still perceive themselves as being all alone.

If You Decide to Seek Counseling

If you are severely depressed, would like some comfort and support and the ear of a good listener, and/or need another opinion about your unique situation, you may decide to seek professional assistance.

Regardless of your reasons for wanting counseling, it's important to remember that seeing a therapist is not a sign of mental illness or weakness. On the contrary, people who seek out therapy tend to be strong people, because they have the courage to ask for help—something that's difficult for many to do.

The process of finding a counselor is a bit like interviewing job applicants, and requires a little homework at a time when you may not feel up to it. The best way to find a good therapist is to ask friends or your family doctor for recommendations for marriage counselors or psychologists. Marriage counselors may charge less than psychologists, but some insurance companies may pay only for the services of a psychologist or psychiatrist, so be sure to check your policy. For those without insurance or state medical aid, ask for a sliding scale or sliding fee. This means, of course, that you will be charged according to your ability to pay. Many therapists will quote their fees over the telephone.

In addition, almost every city has a community health center listed in the telephone book, providing low-cost counseling to residents. Many of these centers furnish competent therapy, although there might be a long waiting list for treatment. Many mental health agencies have crisis counselors who see a client one, two, or three times during the crisis, and then schedule the client with another counselor in the same agency if more extensive treatment is appropriate.

It is important to have good rapport with the counselor. The relationship you eventually form should be strictly confidential and completely honest. If you're not at ease with him or her by the second session, discuss your discomfort openly with the therapist. If things don't improve, you may want to look around for another therapist. Remember, however, that your discomfort may have nothing to do with the therapist. It may come from your own pain in looking at things you'd prefer to be able to forget. Counseling is not always fun, but it is healing.

For many there still remains an aura of mystery surrounding seeing a counselor. Counseling today is usually short-term (less than a year, at most) and is focused primarily on current feelings and situations. When you walk into the counseling office you should expect to be treated with dignity and warmth. Intimidation—sometimes called confrontive therapy—is largely a thing of the past. The goal of the therapy is to help you understand and feel good about yourself. For this reason, counseling is appropriate at any stage of your custody crisis.

Action and Identity

When we get depressed, we tend to feel that there's nothing we can do to help ourselves. We can't see anything but our own problems and misery and lose our objectivity, and with it, the ability to pull ourselves out of the slump we're in. We wait until we feel like getting out of bed and getting dressed, for instance. What we don't realize is that *behavior change precedes emotional and attitudinal changes* when it comes to depression. In other words, if you force yourself to get out of bed and get dressed, then you will feel better—not the other way around.

The good news is that depressed people respond quickly to activities which they find personally valuable and life-enhancing—going to night school, writing for profit or pleasure, investing in the stock market, attending or putting on seminars, learning a new skill, making a new friend, improving and redecorating their living or work space, and on and on. Often the activity is something really different, some new direction or avenue, a new dimension of that person. This is not insignificant. To be without our children for most of the week, or most of the year, was once something that seemed unthinkable. To move on with our lives, we have to contemplate the unthinkable—that we can be happy and productive and have a first-rate relationship with our children without custody or with reduced custody. This requires some creativity and looking at options we've never explored before; perhaps we've never given ourselves permission to explore them. In turn, these explorations recharge our emotional batteries, improving our feelings of self-worth, our relationship with our children, and, often, guiding us along more rewarding career paths. So, deliberate action and creative rethinking of who we are—these are the keys to moving out of depression.

"It seemed like I cried for a year straight after my boys moved in with my ex-husband," Carolyn, a stunning blue-eyed brunette, recalled. "It didn't seem like anything could make me feel better. I felt so, so empty that whole first year."

When Carolyn and her well-to-do husband divorced four years before, she was given primary physical custody of their three sons. Two months later, she met Craig and after dating for several months, they decided to move in together. Carolyn's mother, worried that Carolyn's ex-husband might object to Carolyn's living arrangements and take the boys away, began pressuring her to marry Craig. Carolyn complied, "mainly to keep my sons," she admitted.

Soon after they were married, Craig lost his job and Carolyn took a part-time job to help meet expenses. In the meantime, the boys visited their father every weekend and had the time of their lives. "Their father treated them to some amusement park or an excursion that I couldn't possibly afford to pay for myself. When they'd come home and I'd insist that they do their homework and go to bed on time, they would act like I was some kind of monster!"

In the meantime, Craig had stopped looking for work and spent his days watching television and drinking beer. He told Carolyn that their dismal living conditions were all her fault. As she began to believe him, her self-esteem sank lower and lower. Finally, after Craig withdrew some money from their bank account without telling her, their rent check bounced and they were evicted. To add to Carolyn's problems, she had just learned she was pregnant with her fourth child.

"I went out right away to find another place to live. I hunted and hunted, but with three kids, one on the way, a husband who refused to work and very little income, no one would rent to us." Carolyn felt she had no choice but to call her ex-husband and ask him to take the boys "for a while."

"I never really admitted to myself that I was letting go of the boys permanently. I think I knew, but I wouldn't consciously admit it to myself," Carolyn said slowly as she bit her lip and closed her eyes tightly. "Had I the chance to do it over, I would have gotten rid of Craig and kept my boys. . . ." Her voice trailed off as she recalled the period after her sons were gone.

"When my daughter Jessica was born six months later, I was so devastated by the loss of my boys that I had a hard time being affectionate with her. It was so hard to have them move out and to realize that there probably was never going to be a financial opportunity for me to have them back. That part gave me the most trouble—the finality of the whole thing. That the boys would probably always live with their father from then on, and I would always have a broken family.

"I was so frustrated at my predicament. I had no options that seemed any good. If I threw out Craig, there'd be no one to watch Jessica while I was at work and then I'd have even worse financial problems. But if I stayed with Craig, I knew my resentment toward him would only grow."

Four months after her custody loss, Carolyn became withdrawn and quiet. "I was trying to hide from my pain," she said. "I'd sleep almost all the time. Even then, I'd cry in my sleep. I was so lonely— I missed my boys so much! The only times I felt alive were when the boys would come over for a visit, but even then I'd feel sad because I knew they'd soon be leaving."

Recalling the relaxation she'd always found in painting, Carolyn picked up a brush one day and painted a farm scene on an old saw blade. She then busily created several other paintings on old, cast-away items.

Carolyn showed them to her mother: "She said I should sell them! I thought she was crazy, but she went with me to the swap meet that weekend, and I sold all but one of my paintings." Inspired and suddenly hopeful, Carolyn threw herself into her painting. Within six months, she was making a small income. Eventually, she was asked to paint a store-front decoration for a Christmas season display. When other orders for window paintings rolled in, Carolyn's self-confidence blossomed.

With her new outlook and a steady income, Carolyn gained the courage to divorce Craig. Three years later, her sons still live with their father, but Carolyn and her daughter have adjusted to living alone, and with Craig gone, the boys are more enthusiastic about visiting on weekends.

Once a victim of her circumstances, Carolyn is now a victor. Through her artwork, she gained control and meaning in her life.

Her avocation/occupation gave her pride, confidence, and joy as well as an income that allows her to be self-supporting. This new sense of self-reliance was, in turn, largely responsible for bringing her out of the grips of depression.

Connie is another mother without custody who realized that only she could take the steps necessary to help lift her depression. A twenty-five-year-old real estate secretary, Connie began showing depressive symptoms three months after her ex-husband was awarded primary custody of their twins. The first sign of her depression was a lack of energy. She felt as if she were on automatic pilot, doing her work mechanically. Her drive and enthusiasm had vanished.

Connie's house soon reflected how she felt. She kept the drapes shut. Clutter was everywhere. Dirty dishes were piled in the sink. Connie simply didn't care. Each night, she'd come home, lock the door and refuse to answer the telephone because there was nobody she wanted to talk to.

Within a month, Connie's depression had taken over much of her life. All she could think about was her children and how much she missed them. At times, she felt completely paralyzed by the emotional pain. She would move slowly and heavily, as if her legs were filled with wet sand. Right up until bedtime and then again first thing in the morning, Connie recalled, she would feel just awful. Her life up until then, she said, had not been easy, but nothing was as bad as losing daily contact with her twins.

Rarely wanting to eat, she preferred instead to sleep: "My dream life is so much better than my real life." Connie finally made the decision to seek professional help.

During the intial interview with a therapist, Connie revealed just how low her self-esteem had dropped. "When I went to that first counseling session, I couldn't say one good thing about myself. It was as if I had become a nonperson—someone with no value and no rights. At that time, I was jealous of the whole world because I truly thought everyone else had it together, and that I was the only person feeling miserable."

Counseling helped crack some of Connie's negative beliefs. Her first therapy assignment was to read a book on assertiveness so she could begin standing up for her rights. Gradually, she started having small successes using her newfound assertiveness.

"The first time I stood up for myself, I felt so good that I smiled for about an hour! I was at the butcher counter at the grocery store. I had stood patiently waiting for help, and this other lady butted right in front of me. Normally, I would've just stood there and fumed over her nerve. But this time, I spoke up! Not mean, not passively—just firmly. I said, 'Excuse me, but I was next.' The butcher and the lady stopped and apologized, and then he helped me instead of her." She flashed a beaming smile of pride.

These initial successes at being assertive led Connie to renegotiate the visitation schedule with her ex-husband; she got the children every weekend instead of every other weekend. Eventually, she began exercising regularly and eating a more nutritious diet. She lost weight, regained energy and found she could concentrate better. Pretty soon, no one had to encourage Connie to continue exercising and eating well. She loved it!

By Connie's fourth month of counseling, her co-workers were commenting on how great she looked. She felt wonderful, too. Even her house reflected Connie's new outlook. She opened the curtains and cleared away the clutter. Both the home and owner were sunny and organized.

She still had her down moments, as we all do. Talking with her children and hearing "I sure miss you, Mommy" brought tears to her eyes. But instead of isolating herself and blaming the world for her misery, Connie could now deal with her sadness in positive ways such as heading for the gym to work off her pain and anger.

"I'm looking forward to each day now when I wake up," Connie says. "I've even enrolled in night school to get my real estate license and that'll mean a big jump in my income eventually. I'm making the best of a situation I never thought I could live with— being without my kids."

Connie not only found ways to become happy and fulfilled in her noncustodial situation; she learned to take personal responsibility for making the best of it. The methods Connie used to lift her depression—short-term therapy, practicing assertiveness, exercising, and learning to take responsibility for her life—can work for other parents as well.

In the long run, depression occurs for a reason. It forces you to slow down and look inward, face the reality of your custody loss and begin to consider your next move. However, despite the fact that it's necessary to go through this process to reach acceptance, it is so painful that many try to avoid their feelings. What we need to do is to focus on the good, without denying the bad. In other words, allow yourself to cry and grieve over the loss of your children. You may be scared that once you start, you'll never be able to stop. But that won't happen. Hiding from your feelings only makes things worse. But at the same time, don't lose sight of the positive things going on in your life. The telephone calls and visits from your children. The free time you now have to explore and grow. The moments when it feels good just to be alive.

Finding a Friend in Emotions: The Channeling Method

An effective therapeutic technique that I call the channeling method illustrates what happens when we avoid our emotions. Many of my clients have adopted the channeling method and report that it helps them to face their troublesome feelings, instead of suppressing them.

To understand the channeling method, it's helpful to first recall a time when you've felt intense fear—in the courtroom perhaps—or deep sorrow—your first Christmas without the children. Recall the incredible power and intensity of those emotions. Now, think about the times you fought to suppress negative emotions such as anger—after your ex-spouse berated you in front of the children—or jealousy—when the kids talked fondly about the new person in your ex-spouse's life. It undoubtedly took as much or more energy to ignore those emotions as it would to have felt them.

Close your eyes and visualize two rivers rushing in opposite directions toward each other down a narrow ravine. One river is your emotions. The other river is the energy used to suppress or fight them. Then visualize these two rushing rivers meeting head-on, and slamming together in huge waves, with water spewing everywhere.

The same thing happens inside of us when the energy of our emotions encounters an equally powerful force—that is, suppression of feelings we think are bad. Because we have not channeled these emotions through their natural course—that is, because we haven't allowed ourselves to feel the full impact of them—we experience painful inner turmoil. Like the river blocked from flowing into the the tranquil lake at the end of its course, we are stymied in a chronic depressive or anxious state.

The channeling method allows us to treat our feelings—even the ones we think are negative—as resources instead of enemies. Allow yourself to feel the full spectrum of your emotions, from joy to sorrow. You can capture and use their energy. As Sheldon Kopp tells us in his classic work, *If You Meet the Buddha on the Road, Kill Him!*: "All of you is worth something, if only you will own it."

Mark had long felt insecure and frustrated during his daughter's visits because he subconsciously worried that he bored her. However, he wouldn't admit his feelings because of his deep-seated belief that only weak men feel insecure. Instead, he buried his insecurities and told himself to "snap out of it." Before long, Mark started to experience stomach pain before each of his daughter's visitations. Once he linked this intestinal discomfort with his concerns about how he would occupy his daughter, he recognized he could no longer fight or deny his feelings. He began discussing his uncertainties about himself as a father with a close friend. Once he realized he no longer had to feel good one hundred percent of the time, and that it was okay to feel vulnerable and insecure sometimes, Mark's stomach didn't bother him anymore. Thus, his gnawing sense of his own imperfection led him to a more realistic and loving relationship with his little girl.

To channel your emotions instead of fighting them:

—Continue with the exercises discussed in chapter 2 for increasing awareness of your feelings.

—Stay aware of your feelings throughout the day, especially in stressful, tense, or upsetting situations when negative feelings are rampant.

—As soon as you notice yourself feeling uncomfortable or in physical discomfort (stomachache or headache, for instance), ask yourself if it has anything to do with how you're feeling.

—Allow yourself to experience whatever emotion is inside you. Let the feeling flow through its natural channel, unobstructed. Don't ignore or tell feelings to go away. Instead, admit to yourself that "I'm feeling (jealous, inadequate, angry, confused, etc.) right now." The freedom comes when you "own" your feelings instead of them owning you.

A note to men: many men discover, as they progress through the custody crisis, that they are uncomfortable in talking about their softer feelings—sadness, loneliness, fear, regret, dependence. They tend to use anger to cover these feelings up. In their provocatively titled book, *Why Can't Men Open Up?*, Steven Naifeh and Gregory

White Smith identify this culturally sanctioned male closedness:

> To be a man means never to give in to emotions. A man may be affected by them, but never controlled, never swept along in their currents. Only by controlling his feelings can he master the threats and challenges of life. Reason, not feelings, should be the master.

Most men, on one level or another, realize the fruitlessness of this ideal. To live life by reason alone is to be a prisoner of your emotions. As Naifeh and Smith conclude, "The open man is a free man." If you learn nothing else from our exploration of the custody crisis, learn that to move forward, you have to examine your feelings, accept them as valid, and, if they are holding you back from growth, gently let them go. Remember the analogy of the rushing river; when it flows through its natural course, it ends peacefully. But trying to contain it requires massive effort and finally results not in control, but in boiling turmoil. Eventually, the dam will burst.

Women aren't given, at birth, the ability to be vulnerable; it's a learned skill. Men usually aren't encouraged to develop this skill. (This is similar to women's uneasiness when they're asked to directly express anger. When women finally overcome the erroneous belief that they "just can't do that," they find that dealing with this "masculine" emotion is the key to much of their griefwork.)

We all know, at some level, when we're hiding from our feelings. A decision to mask, ignore, channel, or exacerbate depression is usually made with some degree of conscious awareness.

You may have noticed how your viewpoint has much to do with whether you're happy or sad. Depression will grow with pessimistic thoughts or when you dwell on the fact that the children aren't there. Sometimes, you can even talk yourself into a full-blown crying spell just by ruminating on "how sad it all is."

Ed was a client who got into the habit of catastrophizing— creating mental images of the worst possible things that could happen to his daughters, who were living with his ex-wife. He'd imagine they were the victims of some accident or abuse at the hands of his ex-wife's boyfriend. Actually, this was a self-protective measure. He was bracing himself just in case tragedy struck. But Ed's elaborate and gory visions of disaster became almost habitual after several months, and soon Ed was drinking every Sunday night to calm himself down after driving the girls back to their mom. When he began calling in sick every Monday morning, his employer gave him an ultimatum—get help or turn in his resignation.

Through counseling, Ed learned to take responsibility for having fanned the flames of his depression and desperation through his horrible and unrealistic scenarios. He adopted a practical solution to resolving his anxiety: "Now, if I start to worry about my girls, I'll pick up the phone and call them. I always find out they're fine, and that stops me from imagining the worst."

Some "Feel Good Now" Exercises

At this stage, it often feels like the sadness will never go away. But, in time, the depression *will* lift, and you will find rewards worth waiting for. Out of the depths will emerge a stronger, more confident person—someone who has survived the painful experience of custody loss, and who has stood up for his or her beliefs, either by fighting for or surrendering custody. After enduring the custody crisis, you will know that you can survive anything.

Fortunately, there are things you can do right now to bring relief to unhappy days.

First, it's important to guard against negative self-talk that leads to guilt and self-blame. Be alert for the little inner voices that tell you:

—I'm no good, or I would have custody of my children.

—I was really stupid (or weak, selfish, etc.) to give up custody so easily.

—I've ruined my children's—or my parents'—lives forever.

—I don't deserve to feel happy without my children.

—I know that my friends would reject me if they knew about my custody situation.

—My kids won't love me anymore.

—They'll end up calling someone else 'Mommy' or 'Daddy' and I won't matter in their lives anymore.

—I'll never see my kids again.

—What's the use of living, without my kids?

One or another of these thoughts has probably occurred to each one of us at some point. In and of themselves, these thoughts serve no purpose. Now, if thinking such things drives you to better your or your children's situation in a way that makes you feel good about yourself, then the guilt and self-recrimination were useful. However, if you simply fall into such thinking as a habit, it may *prevent* you from improving things. Once you convince yourself you're worthless, you will also convince yourself that there's nothing such a worthless person can do to be a better parent or a better person.

We often behave as if we are helpless against our own thoughts, but thought-stopping is a long-recognized and effective therapeutic technique. If you find negative thoughts running through your mind, tell these thoughts to "STOP!" You can do this by literally screaming "stop!" or just by thinking the word to yourself. The more dramatic you can make the process of telling yourself to stop the negative self-talk, the better. Some try putting rubber bands around their wrists and then snapping them each time a negative thought creeps into their awareness.

As soon as you tell yourself to stop the negative thought, replace it with a positive one. This could include one of the following:

—I am a good parent.

—I'm the only qualified judge of whether my custody situation is right for me, or not.

—The custody arrangement is the best thing for the children, even if they can't understand that right now.

—It's too bad that my parents don't agree with my decision to surrender custody, but I just can't live my life to please them.

—I deserve to feel happiness, with or without my children. Life is too short to put joy and pleasure 'on hold.'

—If I'm unhappy with my current situation, I'll take positive action to improve it.

—It's important that I feel good about myself. In the long run, I'm a better person and parent for keeping up my self-esteem.

—I'll work hard to keep up a strong, loving relationship with my children.

In addition to deliberately replacing negative self-talk with positive and uplifting affirmations, a variety of activities can help parents maintain a healthy level of self-esteem and decrease depression. To begin with, we need to take good care of ourselves to feel good about who we are. This includes getting enough sleep, exercise, and eating balanced meals. But even more, it means pampering ourselves. Following divorce and custody loss, people often feel very lonely. There may be no one at home who cares about them. No one to buy them gifts or boost their egos. So, at least for a time, it's the parents' sacred responsibility to be good to themselves.

Try to have at least one positive experience every day. You deserve it! And if you don't believe that right now, you *will* begin to believe it if you start to take care of yourself and allow yourself to have fun. Here are some suggestions:

—Rediscover the beauty and serenity in nature. Spend at least one-half hour each day admiring a sunset or garden or even better, actively engage yourself in nature by planting a flower bed or putting up a birdhouse.

—Get a new haircut. Or a manicure. How about a massage? Even an occasional long, hot, undisturbed bath is great for self-pampering.

—Treat yourself as you would a welcome guest. Eat meals on your best dinnerware. Keep green plants or fresh flowers around your home. Buy that new "toy" you've been wanting to get—a camera, a fishing pole, a bicycle—something that takes you outside to play. Start saving for that long overdue vacation. Get full service at the gas station occasionally and now and then buy the best brand of your favorite foods instead of the plain wrap variety. Be good to yourself and your inner self will believe that you are a worthwhile person. You don't need other people to boost your self-esteem for you.

—Join a health club, YMCA or YWCA and slowly but regularly get yourself into good physical shape. Studies have shown that regular exercise is as effective for alleviating mild depression as short-term counseling! You'll feel proud with each new "rep" or "set" you add to your exercise routine, and this is also an excellent way to meet new people.

—Do you have a secret ambition that feels impossible or unrealistic? Maybe it's time to think about making that idea come to fruition. Write down your "wish list" of life goals.

Whether you want to write a book, climb a mountain, go to business, law or medical school, or move to a beach house, begin thinking in terms of possibilities and small steps you can take right now to realize even your wildest dream.

—Remind yourself, every day, "I deserve to be happy."

6
Toward Hope, Acceptance, and Serenity

*The only way I've been able to accept the fact
that my son lives with my ex-wife is to keep
telling myself over and over that he's better off
this way. And I know he is. I just sometimes
remember how miserable I was with her and I
guess I get my own feelings mixed up with my
son's. Anyway—sometimes I have to swallow
my pride to admit this—everybody's really
much better off this way.*
> —Thirty-four-year-old father,
> three years after losing custody
> of his son

As the weeks and months after custody loss pass, the custody crisis brings the parent to a fork in the road. At this point, a choice must be made: will he or she bury the emotional pain of losing custody, or withstand some psychological discomfort in order to find serenity in acceptance?

Not everyone reaches the stage of considering acceptance, because, as we've seen, just getting to this stage takes pain, struggle, and work. Many, understandably, put their grief on hold. They may remain blindly stuck in one of the stages. Some run the gamut of emotions: they're shocked, angry, frightened, and/or sad, sometimes in recurring cycles. Acceptance seems like an impossibly high hurdle. Typically, they try to behave as if it were all a bad dream. They try to block out thoughts of the children or refuse to admit the custody loss to themselves or anyone else.

Lena came to me for therapy after she was fired for the second time in a year. Although during our first session it appeared that

Lena was suffering from depression, it turned out that she was holding onto intense rage that soured every personal and business relationship in which she became involved. Lena said she knew that people were repelled by some part of her personality, but she couldn't figure out what it was.

I could see what it was that pushed others away from her. Lena was so bitter, so full of what can only be called hate that she was frightening to be around. There were times, in our initial sessions, when I fully expected her to start verbally assaulting me. Others, probably out of self-protection, avoided her. At worst, they disliked and persecuted her, which had led to her two job dismissals. It took a while for Lena to become aware of the extent of her anger, and the way it was seeping into the way she talked and carried herself. Since Lena had been raised to believe that anger was a "sinful" emotion, she wouldn't allow herself to see how much of it was within her. We traced her current anger back to Lena's custody loss two years before. She was still fuming over what she considered the unjust way the trial was handled. Every time she got in touch with this anger, she felt guilty.

"It was like my mother was sitting on my shoulder watching me and lecturing me about how 'unladylike' and evil anger is," she later recounted. "So, I had no choice—at least I felt I had no choice then—but to hold all that anger in, inside of me."

Lena was also afraid that she'd lose control if she allowed herself to express her anger: "It just felt like there was a volcano in me waiting to explode." Assertiveness training played a big part in her therapy, allowing her a constructive outlet for this pent-up anger. Once she had let off a great deal of steam about her custody loss, we began working on other grief issues, including sadness. After five months of weekly therapy, Lena was no longer stuck in her anger and seemed to have come to an acceptance of her loss, after two years of getting nowhere. Her assertiveness certainly helped to hasten her acceptance; through it, she was able to obtain additional visitation time from her ex-husband—a factor which increased her satisfaction with the custody arrangement.

The Possibility of Acceptance

Unlike the other stages of the custody crisis, acceptance doesn't powerfully overtake you. Instead, you must approach it yourself.

Within the struggle to accept, we can visualize three "sub-stages." Let's call them the early, middle and late phases of acceptance. In the early phase, we give the idea of acceptance some thought. Perhaps our friends have told us to quit worrying and let the thoughts about custody go. Or maybe we've read about grieving and learned that acceptance is a goal or a challenge to be accomplished. We're resistant to doing much more than pondering what it would be like to accept the loss. We're not emotionally ready to face the possibility of acceptance, because it feels too risky, as if we are admitting that we *like* our custody arrangements.

In the middle phase, we feel a bit weary of the negativity which has characterized much of the custody crisis. We long for a return to the attitude that life in general is very good. We long to become alive to the world again, and for the world to become alive to us.

We may be accustomed to the visitation schedules by the middle phase, and the custody arrangement has been integrated as a steady routine. We move from rigid standpoints to more flexible thinking. The possibility of compromise and a happy, or at least moderately happy, outcome for both parents is considered. Issues of guilt are addressed as we think, "Will my children think I don't love them if I accept this custody arrangement?"

In the final phase, we come as close as we can to acceptance. This is not a resting place. Acceptance is more of a daily balancing act, requiring reaffirmation of our positive beliefs about the custody arrangement and allowing, finally, some inner peace after months or years of inner turmoil.

This acceptance means being able to look back on the days before the loss and having feelings of joy for *what we once had*— feelings that are stronger than the sadness for what is now lost. We are able to remember the days when our children lived with us full-time and feel, "I'm so glad I had that." That feeling—once acceptance has occurred—will overshadow, though not erase, the emotional pain of losing custody.

Acceptance does not mean, as some may believe, "caving in," or going over to the enemy camp. It also does not entail giving up hope that custody may one day be regained. You don't have to like your noncustodial, or infrequent-access, status in order to accept it. Rather, acceptance signifies being able to live with the loss, even if another attempt to gain custody is planned for the future. The by-products of being able to accept life without custody are peace of mind and emotional well-being.

But knowing when you have, in fact, reached a level of acceptance requires a great deal of self-honesty. It's so easy to regard griefwork as a sort of competition with oneself, reaching for the finish line of acceptance. With that mind-set, the emotions which we need to work through are rushed over.

Acceptance can't be rushed. Most grief experts agree that it takes a minimum of six months before the various stages of grief can be worked through. And, acceptance is not a one-shot experience; it is a lifelong process. Anger, fear, sorrow and regret will arise over the years, and some of the depression triggers discussed in chapter 5 will not lose their power.

The Tale of the Happy Ending

As children we firmly believed that every story had a happy ending. This myth made for great fairy tales and Saturday morning cartoons, and most of us raised on a steady diet of characters who "lived happily ever after" began to expect that we would do the same in our adult lives.

For many parents, losing custody may be the first time they've experienced a major loss. They are tormented by the belief that this just isn't the way life was supposed to turn out. They are unprepared for the intense emotions of the custody crisis, have no idea how to deal with them, and suspect their feelings are abnormal.

A lot has been written about the way our society has largely lost touch with grieving skills. As recently as the turn of this century, several generations lived under the same roof; this meant death and loss were witnessed up close with "grief counseling" provided by other relatives. Family members learned at a young age that loss is a part of life.

Today, people live longer, and our first experience with the death of a loved one may not occur until we are forty or fifty years old. Death is softened by euphemisms, we don't hold wakes anymore, and the business of caring for the dead body has been handed over to funeral homes. The whole concept of death is kept on an unemotional, surrealistic level. Unfortunately, many of us are therefore ill-prepared to accept and deal with natural grief reactions.

Another attitude that affects our reactions to loss springs from our "throw-away" culture in which possessions are expected to wear out and need replacing. Nothing, it seems, is designed for permanent use. This makes it difficult to accept a permanent loss, because of the expectation that everything lost can be replaced. We aren't conditioned to accept that something, someone or some situation is beyond repair. Thus, when a family is torn apart by divorce, our inclination is to deny its finality. We protest, "No, this can't be true! There must be something I can do to fix it!"

New Attitudes

Is life unfair to parents who lose custody of their children? How responsible is the parent for losing custody? Every person must answer these questions for him- or herself. There are some viewpoints, however, that may offer parents comfort and a fresh perspective.

In his book, *Man's Search for Meaning,* psychiatrist Viktor Frankl describes a philosophy that is readily applicable to the custody crisis: Despite anything the world renders—good or bad— you always have the choice of what attitude to hold. In other words, you are free to find either positives or negatives in any circumstance.

Not only does Frankl dispute the traditional notion of equating happiness with a problem-free existence, he also sees a balance of personal free will in accepting those things we cannot change. He writes, "When we are no longer able to change a situation—just think of an incurable disease such as inoperable cancer—we are challenged to change ourselves."

Frankl's philosophy, as applied to the custody crisis, asks us to either change a negative situation or change the way we view it. If you're unhappy that your ex-spouse was awarded primary physical custody of the children, you have three basic choices on how to deal with it. First, you can remain angry, unhappy and unsettled about the custody loss. Or, you can try to change it by going back to court (we will address this possibility in chapter 10). Finally, you can change the way you think and feel about the custody loss by finding good in it somehow and learning to accept.

None of the choices is easy. The third choice, attitude change, requires you to focus on the positive by noticing, for instance, that your children's school grades are improving, or how your kids seem to smile more often. This doesn't mean you should overlook serious warning signs in the name of optimism. If your children are well-treated by your ex-spouse, you can help yourself by asking "what's *good* about this situation?'' instead of paying attention only to the negatives.

I think of Tami, who surrendered custody of her son to her ex-husband fifteen years ago. She proudly discusses how well Bill, now twenty-five, is doing. "He has a fantastic career and a wonderful wife. . . . If I had tried to raise Bill by myself, he wouldn't have gotten all the advantages that my husband could afford to provide. You know, a good private school and tuition, that kind of thing. God knows I did the best thing for Bill when I let him live with my ex-husband after our divorce." For Tami, acceptance of the loss was the result of continually keeping in mind what was best for her child. This included actively keeping alive her relationship with her son.

To psychologist, philosopher and author Rollo May, the ability to face conflict ensures our personal freedom. He writes in *Psychology and the Human Dilemma*,

> To be free means to face and bear anxiety; to run away from anxiety means automatically to surrender one's freedom. Demagogues throughout history have used the latter strategy—the subjecting of people to continuous unbearable anxiety—as a method of forcing them to surrender their freedom. The people may then accept virtual slavery in the hope of getting rid of anxiety.

This view of conflict differs from most people's attitudes toward opposition and struggle. There has been a collective choice to view conflict as negative, to be avoided or disposed of as quickly as possible. Frankl and May would have us, instead, see the custody crisis as an opportunity to gain new meaning, acquire new interpersonal skills and grow in new directions.

The Chinese pictogram for the word "crisis" is a combination of two symbols: "danger" and "opportunity." The danger of the custody crisis—the emotional pain experienced by parent and child, the inability to forgive ourselves and others, the possibility of becoming embittered and emotionally stifled—has been discussed throughout this book. The *opportunity* that comes with the custody crisis is more subtle and holds different meanings for each person.

This I know—acceptance brings growth. As we reacquaint ourselves with the comfort that faith brings, either through a connection to a church or synagogue, or through personal beliefs and meditation, spiritual growth occurs. As we stop kicking ourselves and start nurturing ourselves, our self-esteem improves and emotional growth occurs. As we learn more about ourselves and our creativity is challenged, we grow intellectually. Many of us will also reluctantly admit that without custody, we have free time which allows us to continue our education, start a new business or pursue new interests—all adding up to growth.

Custody loss may be the most difficult and painful situation you have ever been forced to endure. No matter what the details involved in your custody case were, the wounds caused by parting with a child go very deep. Yet, after facing the challenge that custody loss forces on us, there is a sense of accomplishment: "I SURVIVED!" This brings to mind the line from philosopher Nietzsche: "That which does not kill me makes me stronger." Once you've been through custody loss, other situations pale in their ability to intimidate or scare you. The custody crisis, then, can leave you a stronger, more confident human being. When acceptance truly occurs, it's the emotional equivalent to climbing the world's tallest mountain.

Since acceptance is an ongoing process, the years that follow that first year of suffering will also bring their own challenges. At times, you will feel so empty that it will seem that you're the only person who has ever felt this inadequate as a person and parent. Rest assured that you are not alone.

At other times, the feel of your child's arms around you will make the pain vanish and you will truly appreciate the "here and now." Appreciate the delicious way that love warms your body and remember how it feels, so that next week, when you're alone again, the memory can comfort you.

Becoming a parent changes a person forever. You will always be the mother or father of your child. There will always be a lasting bond of caring and love between you and your son or daughter. Custody loss cannot change that. You and your children, through your separation, may come to appreciate one another even more. You'll still have jokes with your child that only the two of you understand. During your visits together, you can still let go, have fun, and pretend to be a kid again. Laughter, whispered secrets, and warm, warm hugs. These are still yours.

And it will be during those moments of love and laughter that you'll feel glad to be alive, glad to be who you are. And very glad to be a parent.

Considering Acceptance

So, accepting your custody arrangements turns the feeling of "I lose" into one of "I love." Acceptance means feeling more relaxed and flexible, and less defensive. Your acceptance will be transmitted to your children and they, in turn, will have a greater chance for a healthy attitude about shared custody arrangements, visitations, and phone calls to or from the other parent. Moreover, the children will want to be with you more as you are more peaceful and accepting.

To help you with your struggle over acceptance, ask yourself the following questions and take as much time as you need to answer them honestly. If you find you are resistant to acceptance, stop and look for reasons why. It will be helpful to go through these questions more than once. Chances are that your responses will change as your custody crisis evolves.

—Acceptance seems impossible to think about because:

—To me, acceptance means that I would experience the following emotions:

—If I accepted my custody arrangement, my thoughts about my custody status would be:

—Acceptance of my current custody situation would mean that my actions and behaviors would be:

—To truly accept my custody arrangement, I'd first have to:

—The most threatening thing about acceptance is:

—Acceptance would be advantageous to me because:

—One good reason to accept my custody arrangement is:

—Another good reason is:

—How would I know if I had begun to accept my custody loss?

—Why am I afraid or reluctant to accept my custody arrangement?

—Am I afraid certain people would misjudge me as uncaring if I accepted my loss? Who are these people? What responses could I give them to assure them and myself that I *am* a caring person?

—Do I think my kids would feel unloved if I accepted the current custody arrangement?

—Do I feel that acceptance signals weakness, failure or giving up?

—Do I feel that acceptance means giving up control?

—How would I feel differently about myself if I accepted my custody loss?

—Would my life be better or worse if I accepted my situation? In what way?

Although we've come to the final stage of the custody crisis, we're in no way finished with discussing all the issues that affect divorced parents. The custody crisis is a dynamic problem—it requires ever-changing responses on an intellectual, behavioral, and emotional level.

In the remaining chapters we'll look at a few of the many, many ways your relationships—with your children, your ex-spouse, your own parents, and others—are affected by the custody crisis. And, we'll examine ways to keep these relationships on a positive course.

7

Helping Your Children through the Custody Crisis

I'd be happier if I didn't even know about the custody case. I wouldn't worry so much and I wouldn't be scared about where I was going to live.

> —Nine-year-old boy discussing his feelings about his parents' second custody battle

When you lose custody of your children, you tend to feel like you've been stripped of your parenthood medals. You wonder just what damage you've done to your children and whether they will ever get over it. You feel you have fallen from a cherished ideal: "I always told myself I'd be such a great parent—now look at me!" But this feeling is usually fleeting. Soon enough you realize that you are still very much responsible for guiding, loving, praising, scolding, laughing with, and crying with your children. It is your immediate and ongoing responsibility to help them cope effectively with the divorce and custody arrangements. There are plenty of triumphs and mistakes to come in your parenting career. Although it may be harder now than it ever has been, the rewards of parenthood are still just as profound.

It is beyond the scope of this book to offer an exhaustive discussion of the psychology and special problems of children of divorced parents. There are many resources available to you on this subject and I've listed some excellent ones in the Suggested Reading section of this book. You should seek them out. In fact, I suspect that you already have; for most of us, reading a book about our own feelings is secondary in importance to learning about how to help our children. However, as you know, my theme is that *helping yourself is helping your children.* One of the best things you can do for them is to proceed with your griefwork while staying carefully attuned to their feelings and needs—their griefwork—and sharing with them what you've learned. Be aware that children also go through the stages of shock, anger, panic, and depression in response to divorce. Grieving together can make your relationship much stronger; in fact, it can make all the difference. Keeping this in mind, I do want to offer some comments on children's perspective of the custody crisis and how I think you can help your children grieve and cope, as well as improve your relationship with them.

Children's Stresses and Symptoms

Concern over "what will happen to me now?" is foremost in children's minds when they find out about their parents' impending divorce. They often feel insecure about their future and frightened of the unknown. As Mom and Dad make preparations for the separation—packing for the move, discussing how and when to sell the house—fear can overwhelm a child. These feelings can be compounded when Mom and Dad, emotionally drained by the situation, neglect to reassure them that they'll still be loved and cared for even though the family will no longer live together.

Children also harbor guilt and shame about divorce as they privately wonder "Did Mom and Dad get a divorce because of me?" If children of any age fail to express those concerns, they loom large and instrusive in their minds. They may try to keep the divorce a secret from schoolmates and friends. They may exhibit the bargaining behaviors we discussed earlier, promising to you, to themselves, or to God, to be good if only you and the other parent will stay together. Be aware that the primary fantasy of children in this situation is that their parents will get back together. Even after having genuinely accepted and declared love for a stepparent, children will routinely express their desire for their family of origin to reunite.

For children, the stress of divorce stems not only from actually witnessing their parents' marriage dissolve, but from the inevitable changes that divorce incurs. Some of these stressful changes are subtle—like not having Mom around to help on a geography project or Dad to fix a broken bicycle. Other changes are drastic. After their parents divorce, children often must move from their home and away from school and friends. They may be struggling with lowered self-esteem and have a difficult time making new friends.

Children who end up living with their mothers are also likely to experience a severe drop in the family's economic status. This means doing without toys, clothes, and activities they used to enjoy, and adds fuel to children's anger over the divorce. A friend related to me the story of a high school senior whose parents were divorcing. The resulting financial bind made it unlikely that her parents could send her in the fall to the college of her dreams, where she had already been accepted. The daughter could take a part-time job, but this in turn would make it almost impossible for the girl to take the rigorous double major she wanted. One day she burst into her mother's place of work, screaming at her in front of boss and co-workers, "You're so selfish! I can't be what I want to be because of your divorce!" Children of divorcing parents get an abrupt lesson in handling disappointment and lowered expectations.

After the divorce, visitations can become an emotionally draining ritual for children. Seven-year-old Bobby said that his frequent shuttling between the homes of his mother and father made him feel like a baseball: "It's like my parents have bats and they hit us back and forth. Mom's the catcher because she's who we stay with, but it makes me mad that we have to always go back and forth like that."

In joint custody and situations in which children spend a more or less equal amount of time with each parent, children often are stressed over the constant traveling and confusion over whether this is the weekend they spend with Mom or Dad. Practical annoyances like forgetting a needed textbook or a pair of tennis shoes plague them as they shuffle between homes. They experience a sense of having lost control. "It's no fair!" said nine-year-old Tracy. "It's my body. How can a judge who's not even part of my family tell me when I have to be with my dad and when I can be with my mom! No one even asks me what I want."

But for many children the most stressful moments during the custody crisis surround the heated battles their mothers and fathers may continue to wage long after the divorce is final. "I thought Mom said these fights would be over after the divorce," the child may wistfully reflect. It can also feel like their parents are pulling them in two different directions when they put children squarely in the midst of disputes or pump them for information. "What kind of dinners does Daddy feed you?" "How often does Mommy take you to the doctor?" The barrage of questions would make anyone's head spin. And when the child intuitively knows that malice toward the other parent underlies these interrogations, the child's loyalties are tested to the limits. Nicole, six, felt so pressured when interrogated by both parents as well as by the various court-appointed counselors investigating her parents' custody battle that she finally became extremely uncooperative whenever anyone asked her anything. "No more questions!" she began screaming one day after her mother inquired about a visit with her dad. "I don't want to answer any more questions!"

Children have a deep, ongoing desire to please *both* parents, to accept and feel accepted by both parents. If a child learns that Mommy loves to hear complaints about how Daddy treats him, he will tell plenty of stories in an effort to gain rewards and attention. But the child will feel confused next time he sees Daddy, because although his mother has validated the idea that Daddy is "bad," the child still experiences him as "good." While he still wants to please Daddy, he experiences conflict over being "two-faced" in his relationship with him.

Further pressure is created if children are asked either subtly or overtly, "Whom do you *really* want to live with?" The child thinks, "I want to live with *this* parent, but if I say so, I risk losing the love of my other parent." Don't assume your children are capable of resolving this kind of anxiety on their own, without reassurance from both parents. Young children cannot say to themselves, "It's too bad that right now Mom doesn't accept that I want to live with Dad, but I know deep down she still loves me. She'll get over it." Being rejected, abandoned, and unloved forever after is a very real fear for children.

A child faces the same dilemma when one parent criticizes the other in the child's presence. The child doesn't want to be disloyal to, or risk losing, either parent. No child was ever helped by the "revelation" that his or her parent is no good. In the same vein, if the child hears that Dad or Mom is no good one minute, and then hears "You're just like your father!" or "You're just like your mother!" the next, the child internalizes that negative judgment.

Of course, children are also hurt very deeply by noncustodial parents who completely disappear from their lives. These kids often blame themselves for the absence of their mothers or fathers, thinking "My dad (or mom) doesn't like me anymore or he (or she) would come to see me." When the parent fails to make child support payments, the child may feel the parent is saying "I don't care about you anymore." Peggy, fourteen, was so angry at her father for never coming to see her, failing to pay child support and causing her mother to struggle to make ends meet, that she entertained fantasies of finding her father so she could beat him up.

Threats of another custody battle are traumatic for children. During every visitation, Angela's mother consistently badgered the little girl about coming to live with her even though the sixth-grader was content being with her father, stepmother and teen-aged brother. But fearing that she'd hurt her mother's feelings if she said outright that she didn't want to move in with her, Angela became increasingly anxious, irritable and tearful as each vistation with her mother approached. This continued for several months until her mother finally ended her efforts to coax the child into living with her. When you and your spouse divorced, your child's sense of stability may have been badly damaged. Be aware of anything you are doing to perpetuate unnecessarily the child's sense of living in limbo.

Parents can inflict emotional pain on their children, usually unintentionally, because their feelings toward their ex-spouses are so overwhelmingly negative. Becky never consciously meant to hurt her six-year-old daughter Brooke. But her unresolved anger toward her ex-husband, Michael, caused her to use the child as a kind of vent for that anger.

Becky referred to Michael as a sex maniac and said that during their marriage he had constantly demanded sex from her. Their marriage had ended when Michael's affair with his secretary came to light. Although there seemed to be nothing suspicious about Michael's behavior toward Brooke, and Brooke was not displaying any physical or emotional symptoms, Becky was convinced that Michael was sexually molesting Brooke and insisted that the little girl be vaginally examined for signs of sexual abuse. When Becky picked Brooke up for visitation every other weekend and alternating holidays, the first activity on her agenda was a trip to the hospital emergency room. Again, she had no evidence whatsoever that her suspicions were well-founded. It seemed her view of Michael was so low that she wouldn't "put anything past him." Although her irrational feelings about Michael could be described as normal for anyone who has just undergone a nasty divorce, her actions on those feelings irresponsibly involved her daughter. Not surprisingly, Brooke soon began showing signs of anxiety, including crying spells and acting out, when she knew it was time for a visitation with her mother.

Michael became worried about his daughter's behavior and took her to a child psychologist. Using play therapy with anatomically correct dolls, the psychologist learned about the vaginal exams and the emergency room personnel's detailed questions. Fortunately, the psychologist was able to convince Becky to stop the emergency room visits. Eventually, Brooke no longer exhibited signs that she was disturbed.

The pressures that children of divorced parents are subjected to often translate into behavioral problems. One third-grade teacher said she can always tell when one of her students is the center of a custody dispute. "The kid will just take a nose dive," she commented. "His grades, mood, concentration and whole behavior will really be off until things at home can even out somewhat. But for kids who have really traumatic visits, things never get better at school. I've come to expect that about half the students in each class I teach will be experiencing divorce-related problems."

Marked changes in the child's behavior at home are also apparent during the custody crisis. Such changes, which are signs of childhood stress and depression, can include bedwetting, extreme aggressiveness, irritability and isolation or introversion. Children also express emotional distress through frequent nightmares.

Physical ailments may also appear. Nine-year-old Renee, who had lived with her father for four years, became tense and anxious after she went to live with her mother. She felt rejected by her father, whose new wife had decided she didn't want children in the house. Renee was also unaccustomed to living in her mother's cramped apartment after the years spent in her father's spacious home. The little girl's stress eventually caused her to suffer extremely painful headaches. Other childhood signs of stress can include digestive problems, sleep disorders and asthma. Parents who notice any such symptoms should consult a pediatrician.

Indications that children may not be adjusting well to their parents' divorce and the subsequent custody arrangements are often apparent when children "act out" before and after visitations. Many mothers and fathers misinterpret this behavior. The noncustodial parent mistakenly assumes that the child who is uncooperative during a visit has been spoiled by the custodial parent. Conversely, the custodial parent assumes the ex-spouse has somehow agitated the child when the youngster throws a tantrum after returning from a visitation.

It is normal for children to act somewhat excited before and after a visit. But you may notice other patterns, such as bedwetting or hitting immediately preceding or following a visitation, which indicate adjustment problems. Gently encourage your child to talk about his or her feelings: "What's troubling you, Johnny?" Avoid using leading questions ("You're afraid to go to Dad's for the weekend, aren't you?"), and if the child's answers are vague, try having him or her draw the feelings connected to the visit. While interpreting the psychological implications of children's artwork is a speciality in itself, you can draw some preliminary conclusions if you consistently see violence, somber colors and/or depressing subject matter in your child's drawings. More information on the subject of talking to your children as well as selecting a good children's counselor appears later in this chapter.

Older children who don't cope well with the custody crisis may find themselves in trouble at school or with the police. Tony, seventeen, had been involved in a brutal fight on his high school campus before entering counseling as a requirement of his parole. While talking with the therapist, Tony revealed that his mother had disappeared shortly after surrendering custody of him to his father when Tony was ten. "I don't blame her for doing it," he said. "I knew before she left that she was really unhappy." Tony insisted that his dad had suffered more from her absence than he had, and that he still loved his mother even though he hadn't seen her since she left.

It became obvious during therapy that Tony thought it would be a terrible mistake to allow himself to feel the hurt that welled up inside him. In fact, the tall, strikingly handsome young man seemed to be exceptionally sensitive to the feelings of everyone except himself. During group therapy sessions, he was keen to point out everyone's else's problems. The key to Tony's healing was in allowing him permission to talk about how he felt.

The point of this quick survey of some of the myriad problems children experience is to show how real their pain is; it goes very deep, and cannot be ignored any more than your own can. They, too, are in the midst of a personal process of pain, awareness, and adjustment. While most parents recognize this, many frequently are so burdened by guilt, self-doubt, and daily stress that they feel helpless to help their children, or don't clearly look at the signs their children are displaying.

The Guilt Crunch

Adrienne softly hung up the telephone, walked into the bathroom, sat down on the edge of the bathtub and began to cry. Her teen-aged son Chad was failing three of his high school classes and the school counselor wanted to see her in person the following day.

"I should've let Bill take Chad after the divorce," Adrienne thought, suddenly feeling totally incompetent as a parent. "None of this would've happened if he had lived with his dad instead of me." She buried her face in a tissue and reflected on the emotional and financial struggles she'd endured to retain custody of Chad. Conflict raged inside her as she debated back and forth: "Chad would probably do better in school if he lived with Bill . . . but how could I give him up—would he ever forgive me?"

After eating dinner during a visitation with her father, four-year-old Rosemary motioned that she wanted more ice cream. "No, Rosie," her father, Gary, said, "you've had enough sugar for one day." The girl suddenly threw her spoon on the floor and began screaming four-letter words at him until he shouted at her to stop.

Gary suspected that Rosemary had learned that language from her mother's new boyfriend. And, he immediately wondered, "Would this have happened if I'd fought for custody like my lawyer wanted me to?"

Kirk spent every summer living with his mother in her high-rise apartment. Things had gone fairly smoothly in the two years since his parents divorced when Kirk was thirteen. His parents had explained that the fighting would now be over and how Kirk would remain in the family house with his father.

Jeanine, Kirk's mother, had graduated from law school the year before the divorce and was settled in an up-and-coming law firm.

She felt ready to spend a pleasant summer with her son. A couple of evenings before they were to leave on a two-week vacation, Jeanine sped home to tell Kirk some good news—a co-worker had offered them the use of his mountain cabin. She rushed excitedly into the apartment only to find Kirk hurriedly snuffing out a marijuana cigarette.

Stunned and furious, she screamed, "How could you!" Kirk was wide-eyed and terrified. A jolt of pain gripped Jeanine's side as she sunk into the sofa. Looking down, all she could think was, "Whose fault is this?"

Whose fault *is* it when children behave in destructive, defiant ways following custody split-ups? Would these behaviors occur if the family had stayed together? Who's more responsible for the child's behavior: the noncustodial or custodial parent? Often these kinds of questions are the focus of a parent whose child is having trouble adjusting after a divorce. Again, there is the need to blame someone or something for our problems, to absolve ourselves, to feel in control, to alleviate that terrible guilt. In the last few pages, we've looked at the severe stresses and problems that children experience when their parents divorce, but it is usually a mistake to use a recent divorce and new custody arrangements as a catch-all to explain all your kids' plus your own problems. Instead, become solution-oriented; *focus on helping your child rather than on finding fault.* First, let's look at the environment you create for your child; then we'll look at two-way communication between you and your child.

How to Help Your Child Thrive

Dr. Dee Sheperd-Look, a licensed clinical child psychologist and professor of psychology at California State University, Northridge, has researched joint custody since 1970. Based on studies of thousands of families, she has identified four conditions necessary for children to thrive in shared-custody arrangements. While her recommendations are related to joint custody, they can be applied to virtually any custodial arrangement.

1. Establish a cooperative relationship with your ex-spouse in matters concerning the children. Despite the resentment you may harbor toward one another even long after the divorce is final, you and your ex-spouse should make every effort to communicate civilly when making decisions concerning your children. "This means parents must learn to control and restrain themselves in order to protect their children," writes Dr. Florence Bienenfeld in her book, *Helping Your Child Succeed After Divorce*; when parents fight, children "never witness it as detached spectators or observers. Because most children are attached to *both* parents, each unkind remark is a blow felt by them. Aside from frightening them and making them miserable, imagine what this teaches them about life and about relationships. The images of this conflict will remain with them forever."

When parents set aside their differences and make every effort to get along, the message the child receives is, "You are more important to me than my being right and Dad (or Mom) being wrong." Children are also more at ease when they sense that decisions about their upbringing are made in their best interests rather than resulting from a power struggle between their parents. Obviously, achieving that kind of cooperative relationship is a challenge, since most couples divorce because they simply can't communicate anymore. See chapter 8.

2. Be sure children have ready access to both parents. This is the second point Dr. Sheperd-Look identifies as being critical. Even when children spend equal amounts of time with each parent, there will be those occasions when they yearn for contact with one parent even though they're on a weekend visit with the other. Some parents angrily regard such contact as an infringement "on my time," especially if it has been weeks since the children's last visitation. Others feel jealous or rejected when youngsters express a momentary preference for the other parent. But if you pause to reflect on when the family was still together, you probably will recall that your children drew different things from you and your ex-spouse. Maybe Mom was the only one who could provide the kind of moral support they needed after a bad day at school. Or perhaps they yearn for the kind of enthusiastic praise only Dad can give after they receive an "A" on a difficult examination. Often these emotional needs don't coincide with the every-other-week-with-Mom (or Dad) arrangement the parents may have worked out so carefully.

When you sense that your child needs to talk to the other parent, you should not view it as rejection on the child's part.

Children naturally crave affection from both mother and father, and their natural yearnings for the other parent are not indicative of whether they love you or not. However, children may run into conflict if they know that their parents are jealous of one another. "I better not tell Mom that I want to talk with Dad. She'll just get upset," the child may conclude. Squelching such needs, of course, is just as unhealthy for children as it is for adults. Communicate to your children that you want and expect them to love, respect, and need their other parent. Have an open-door policy concerning contact with the other parent, and let children know that it's okay to call, write or see Mom or Dad whenever they need to.

In one family I know, the noncustodial father provides his twin girls with pre-addressed, stamped postcards and envelopes so they can write to him regularly. In addition to sending letters himself, he also makes cassette tapes—talking letters—for the girls.

When children are older, mothers and fathers may want to provide the kind of choices that Richard and his brother Kenny enjoy in determining how much contact they have with each parent. Though Kenny, twelve, lives with his mother and Richard, sixteen, resides with his dad, each boy has the choice of where he'll spend his weekends, holidays and vacations. Richard says that because he's relieved of the stress of feeling like he's choosing sides, he can invest his energies into earning good grades and succeeding in sports.

3. Provide children with their own space. Even if your children spend only four or five days a month with you, you should strive to provide them with more than a couch to sleep on, if at all possible. That doesn't mean you need to spring for an entire bedroom set for each child. Sometimes children need only their own twin bed in the corner of a spare room to make them feel they belong.

Gretchen and her second husband, Frank, maintain a spare bedroom in their house especially for Gretchen's son to stay during his visitations. Gretchen and Frank readily acknowledge that they could really use the room for sewing or guests when Jason isn't staying over, but both feel it's important that the room be used exclusively for Jason. "We don't want him to feel like an afterthought when he comes over," the noncustodial mother said. "Jason needs to know that he's as much a member of this household as Frank and myself." Youngsters should also feel free to regard even the most temporary residence as their home. They should be able to fix themselves something to eat or get a glass of water—the normal things they do at their primary residence.

4. *Make every attempt to establish basic philosophies on how children are raised.* While you won't always see eye-to-eye on whether a child should try out for soccer or go to camp for the summer, you should strive to agree on major issues about how the children will be raised. Such agreement provides children with consistency, which is important for several reasons.

Firstly, if the children are faced with one set of rules at Mom's house and another set at Dad's, they're likely to become confused and maybe even disrespectful as they doubt the validity of *anyone's* rules. Inconsistency can also make children feel insecure and unsafe because they're not sure what's expected of them. They don't know which behaviors will bring punishment and which will yield praise. They feel jumpy, perhaps guilty, as they wonder when the axe will next fall on them.

Secondly, if parents hold widely disparate beliefs, their children will likely act out before and after visitations as they try to reconcile and adjust to the different sets of rules with each parent. If, for example, Jimmy is allowed to play outside until 8:30 P.M. when he visits his father on the weekends, when he goes home, Jimmy may consistently rebel against his 8:00 P.M. bedtime. As a result, Sunday and Monday nights will be a constant source of strife between Jimmy and his mother.

Donny experiences similar adjustment difficulties because his parents hold different rules about school and homework. The eleven-year-old lives with each parent six months out of the year. Since Donny's mother and father live in the same city, he is able to attend the same school no matter which parent he stays with. His schoolwork, however, is another matter.

Donny's father, an engineer with a master's degree, puts a great deal of value in education. When Donny lives with his father, he must begin his homework as soon as he comes home from school. No baseball, television or friends are ever allowed to come before his studies. His father spends time each evening explaining difficult math or science problems to Donny and tutors him regularly.

When Donny goes to live with his mother, he keeps up his rigorous study habits for a month or two, but finds it difficult to resist the appeal of sports and pals for much longer than that.

Donny's mother considers her ex-husband's emphasis on homework and grades to be extreme. She doesn't push Donny to finish his homework.

Donny's values and occupational goals fluctuate with his different residences. While Donny isn't experiencing any major difficulties at school at this time, he is starting to distrust his own opinions and beliefs. "I keep changing my mind, so I never can trust what I think," Donny admitted to a teacher who had become concerned about Donny's inconsistent work habits.

It's a good idea to discuss such childrearing differences directly with your children to help them adjust. Tell your child, "I know that at Mom's (or Dad's) you can eat candy before breakfast in the morning, but I have strong feelings about this subject. It's important to me and I want to tell you why." Then discuss those feelings and listen to your child in turn.

Also ask yourself how important the issue really is to you. Is the difference between an 8 P.M. bedtime and a 9 P.M. bedtime having a big effect on the child or very little effect? Be willing to compromise; don't let the phrase, "It's the principle of the thing" allow unimportant issues to make all your lives unpleasant. Reserve insisting that you have a say for the things that you feel are extremely important—perhaps, for example, what religion to bring the child up in. Even then, you might agree that the child go to your place of worship every other week and another on the alternate weeks. Many of these issues—bedtime, homework, extracurricular activities, religious instruction—are tied to your child's age and socioemotional development. Keep in mind your child's personal wishes and responsibilities. Let your child make age-appropriate decisions for him- or herself and don't let responsibilities that really belong to the child become a pointless bone of contention between you and your ex-spouse.

In addition, talk to your ex-spouse about your worries and concerns. It may feel like your ex-spouse is winning and you are losing if you compromise a lot. So you may be tempted to play games to defeat one another. Remember that your goal is to help your child thrive, so compromising to attain that end *is* winning. Don't be afraid to continually remind the other parent of the benefits of cooperation: namely, your child's healthy adjustment to the divorce. It's okay to say things like, "Gee, it feels awkward trying to agree on Johnny's schoolwork when we rarely saw eye-to-eye on this subject when we were married," or, "I can tell this is difficult for you to discuss with me, and it is for me, too," or, "I think it's great that we're able to set aside our differences for Susie's sake."

To sum up, in this emotionally charged situation, try to keep these four principles in the forefront of your mind: Restrain any animosity toward your ex-spouse when discussing the children and don't fight in front of the children; encourage a loving relationship between your children and your ex-spouse; make your children feel at home at your residence; try to come to an agreement with your ex-spouse regarding basic aspects of raising the children and be willing to compromise if the children's best interests will be served.

The Open Door between You and Your Children

Children must be allowed to express their feelings of anger, disappointment, and fear. In the same way that you've learned to tune into your own feelings, you should encourage your children to tune into theirs. In their book *If You Really Loved Me*, Drs. Jordan and Margaret Paul emphasize this point:

> Many children stop sharing their feelings when they feel disapproved for them. But it's not only critical responses that tell children their feelings are wrong. Discounting feelings—"It's really nothing to get so upset about"—or trying to make feelings go away—"Don't feel bad, tomorrow we're going to get you a new puppy"—also communicates to children that their feelings are wrong. Allowing children to feel their feelings deeply while nurturing them communicates that "Your feelings are okay, it's okay to express them, and we have confidence that you can feel them deeply and be all right."

The initial moments of seeing your kids after they have been with the other parent can be awkward, with the kids not knowing what or what not to say. They may have been coached by the other parent on what they shouldn't talk about. You may be tempted to ask a lot of questions to get the conversation rolling. But your children may interpret your eagerness as pressure to reveal secrets. While it's important to remain informed as to how the child is adjusting and being treated, avoid interrogating him or her. Notice the vast difference between saying "What did Mommy do to you?" and "It seems like you're angry about something. Do you want to talk about how you feel?" Better still would be an open-ended question or a nonquestion such as "What happened to make you feel angry?" or, "If you want to talk about it now or later, I'm here to listen." When you ask your child a question, it's important to remain unattached to the outcome. The child may very well say, "No, I don't want to talk about it." But at least you have created an atmosphere of empathy and trust, and the child may come to you later of his or her own accord. If you demand that the child answer you on cue or you expect a certain answer in advance, you are manipulating your child. And of course, children know when they're being manipulated.

At the beginning of a visitation, you can say something like this to your child: "I'm really interested in what you've been doing. Please let me know, when you feel like it, about some of the things that you do. I'd love to listen to you tell about them." This gives the child a greater sense of security about opening up to you. It is understood that the door is open, and that it's up to the child to walk in. The child is reassured that when he or she is ready to talk, the parent will listen without criticism or ridicule (two great fears of children).

Children respond readily to this open-door approach, and will be more communicative if they know that they can talk on any subject when they are ready and that they will be listened to without being interrupted, judged or punished.

At the same time, you should make a consistent effort to tell your children your own feelings. Many of us tend to believe that, as parents, we must appear perfect. When a child asks us a question, we don't feel comfortable answering, "I don't know." We are afraid that our children cannot handle it if we tell them, "I'm scared right now." Drs. Jordan and Margaret Paul have this to say:

> Many children are afraid to express and expose themselves to their parents because they feel it's always one-sided—their parents never let them in on their own difficulties with work, friends, spouse. Children often feel one down and inadequate when they think they're the only ones with problems. This is the major way that people develop the belief that it's wrong to be frightened, sad, disappointed. In addition, when parents don't share their problems and take responsibility for them, children often conclude that the parents' problems are their fault. So sharing your own difficulties and concerns is one way to help them begin to open up.

This is not to say that you should treat your child like an adult friend or therapist; your child is naturally dependent on you, but you should not be dependent on your child to fulfill your emotional needs and understand your problems in depth. Rather, you want to model to your children the act of talking about how you feel. Show them that we feel better after talking about how we feel. It is through this process of genuine sharing with your child that you get to know each other as unique individuals. On this foundation of understanding one another's thoughts, hopes and fears you build a lifelong friendship with this person—your child—who is both part of you and separate from you.

If you haven't had an open-door policy with your children, begin today. If your child is, say, under eight or nine, and especially if he or she is introverted or hesitant, again try drawing. Take a big pad of blank paper and crayons or markers and lie down on the floor with your child. Have some fun. Don't approach this as an exercise that must be completed. Be open-minded and nonjudgmental. Once your child becomes accustomed to telling his or her feelings, he or she will very probably say some things you didn't know, don't want to hear, and which threaten you. But understanding someone means accepting, if not liking, both the good and the bad, and really listening means putting aside your own fears and prejudices. The quickest way to close the door is to invalidate what the child is telling you by criticizing or minimizing.

To begin, draw something symbolic of how you feel, and say (naturally, in age-appropriate language) something like, "Here's a big yellow sun. This is how I am right now, because I feel warm and cheery, and I also feel big and happy. See that big smile on the sun's face. She's happy because she knows how much I love you." Or, "This picture of a big black cloud shows how I feel sad right now. These raindrops I'm drawing are like the tears that I feel inside of me. I'm sad because I know in a few hours I'll have to take you back home and I already miss you."

Then hand the child the crayons and ask him or her to draw the way he or she feels. Ask for an explanation about what the drawing means. However, be careful not to turn the experience into a lecture. You want to stay on an even level with your child during this discussion. You want your child to feel it's safe to talk about the most vulnerable and scary feelings. Don't give the child advice. Give your support. Give your genuine understanding. Give hugs. And give your full attention—this is what your child wants and needs from you.

With pre-teens and adolescents, an easy way to discuss buried feelings is through the language of music and movies. When I'm working with adolescent clients, I spend a lot of time asking them about their favorite songs, movies, and TV shows. I'll ask, "How does this song make you feel?," "What did you like best about the movie?," "What are some of the things you like to see happen on this show?" Then I'll listen quietly, without interrupting, to their answers. Many of their feelings come up in these discussions: anguish over not being handsome, pretty, thin, muscular, smart or rich enough. Mixed feelings about parents. Worries about the future. Try taking your pre-teen or teen-ager to a record store and offering to buy him or her an album, but this time ask what qualities he or she looks for when making a purchase. Or let your adolescent pick out a movie to go to, and then talk about how he or she felt about the story and which characters he or she identified with.

During these talks about feelings, be honest. Don't walk on eggshells, trying to pretend you understand when you really don't or trying to please the child. Your insincerity will be intuitively felt and the child will distrust you. Express your own feelings without putting blame on the child: "I hear you saying that you think I don't trust you, but I don't really understand. What have I done to make you feel that way?" In this process, your child will be learning about his or her feelings, and you, too, will be learning about your feelings and your behavior as a parent.

Again, I must add a fairly strong statement about counseling for children. It's hard to imagine a situation in which a child of divorcing or divorced parents wouldn't benefit from at least a little counseling. If you have a therapist yourself, ask him or her for recommendations. It's usually best to take your child to a mental health professional specializing in the treatment of children and/or adolescents. This could be a psychotherapist (M.A. in psychology or education), a psychologist (Ph.D. in psychology), or a marriage, family, and child counselor (M.F.C.C.). If you don't have a therapist, ask friends who do have a therapist they like and call that therapist for a recommendation, ask your pediatrician for a referral, or use your local physician/counselor-referral service. A psychiatrist isn't usually the best first choice for treating a child unless severe behavioral problems exist. If in doubt, ask your pediatrician.

The counselor will usually want to see your child alone in sessions that last about an hour, two to four times a month. At some point, it may be helpful for you and your child to talk to the therapist together. In my experience, age is related to the total length of treatment. Younger clients usually require fewer sessions than older ones.

Your child should like the therapist and should look forward to the majority of the sessions. While therapy is not for your child's entertainment, it should be a positive experience that he or she enjoys. If not—if your child seems to balk when it's time to go to the session—express your concern to the therapist. If things seem unlikely to improve, then change therapists.

Tips for Least-Access Parents

Finally, a few words to the man or woman who is trying to parent a child he or she sees infrequently.

Sometimes out of guilt and sometimes just because they're trying too hard to make their children's lives pleasant, parents without primary physical custody become "Disneyland Mommies" or "Disneyland Daddies," showering their kids with gifts and extravagant trips during visitations. (As I mentioned back in chapter 3, this can also be a way for a parent to get back at his or her ex-spouse, saying, "See, I'm a better parent than you.")

Lavishing gifts and entertainment on your kids has several drawbacks beyond the fact that it's expensive. First, it creates unreal expectations in children's minds. They begin assuming they'll always be treated royally at the noncustodial parent's home and often they stop appreciating the special treatment. The child may obsess about living with the noncustodial parent, believing that it would be almost as good as living at Disneyland! The youngster may not realize that life has its mundane moments anywhere he or she might live. When children return to their primary home after a luxurious weekend with the noncustodial parent, they may have trouble settling into less exciting but necessary routines. They don't want to get their homework and chores done and their eyes glaze over at talk of learning to be responsible, because they seem to have their other parent's permission *not* to be responsible. Lastly, when the relationship between the noncustodial parent and the child is based on fun derived from external sources like amusement parks and toystores, a void may develop between them. The fun and intimacy that come from sharing thoughts, feelings, and yes, fears, are passed over. *Every visitation ought to contain some time to just sit down and freely talk, with no other distractions, with each of your children, separately. Each child needs that special time alone with you.*

One of the most frequently expressed concerns of noncustodial parents seems to center around their deep fear that "I won't matter in my child's life anymore." One part of this anxiety involves the parent's sincere concern for the child's welfare. Another part of the fear, however, seems to spring from a panic that the need to parent—to raise, teach, enjoy, watch one's child and pass along one's knowledge—will never be met once custody is lost.

Dr. Dee Sheperd-Look relates that in many instances, noncustodial parents are clearly the most significant people and role models in their children's lives. "Depth and quality of relationships are not always built on the amount of time the parent and child are together," she notes. To demonstrate this, she asks us to think back to our own childhoods and recall a significant person in our lives with whom we had infrequent contact. Almost all of us can recall someone—an aunt or uncle or a special teacher—who had a profoundly positive impact on our lives, even though we may have had very little contact with that person. Dr. Sheperd-Look then asks us to remember the type of relationship we had with this special person. Often, this was the only person in our lives who really listened without judging.

This is really the crux of noncustodial parenthood. We all desperately need to be understood by at least one person. If your child truly feels understood by you, you won't lose your influence on him or her. On the contrary, your relationship will thrive, even long distance. This is the kind of relationship you should seek with your children: honest, up-front, warm, and above all, loving.

To achieve this, let's review some of the principles of relating positively with your child. Dr. Florence Bienenfeld provides a succinct checklist in *Helping Your Child Succeed After Divorce*:

1. Become a good listener.
2. Allow your child to express feelings, even hostile, angry feelings and allow him or her to cry.
3. Comfort and reassure your child when he or she is upset.
4. Be demonstrative—show affection for your child.
5. Protect your child from parental disputes or disagreements.

6. Set reasonable rules and limits for your child's behavior according to his or her age and development.
7. Along with discipline, give your child as much praise as you can.
8. Do not call your child names or use put-downs.
9. Set realistic goals for your child and try not to have unrealistic expectations based on what *you* wanted out of life.
10. Avoid excessive behavior, especially drug use and alcohol abuse, around your child.
11. Spend some leisure time and play with your child.
12. Gradually, patiently, and with love, help your child to learn and grow in knowledge, skills, and independence as he or she is ready.

8
Sharing Custody and Parenthood: Your Relationship with Your Ex-Spouse

I find that when I'm with my ex-husband, I have to keep biting my tongue all the time to keep from getting into a fight with him. I bend over backwards to avoid getting into arguments with him, but only for the sake of the kids. I figure they went through too much of our fighting when we were married, and I refuse to put them through any more. But it gets tiring being the one who always compromises.

> —Thirty-five-year-old woman with joint custody of her son and daughter, who live with her during the school year and with their father during summer vacation

Children play an incredibly powerful role in determining their parents' postdivorce relationship. When a childless couple divorces, they often go their separate ways and rarely have cause to interact again. When a couple with children splits up, their relationship will continue by virtue of the ties they have to the children.

There will be visitations and custody arrangements to coordinate. Holidays and birthdays to plan for. Determining whether a child should have braces. And even after the children reach adulthood, divorced parents will probably still cross paths at weddings, graduations and get-togethers. When the children later have their own children, grandparenthood means that the divorced man and woman will continue to see each other at grandchildren's birthday parties and christenings.

Since you and your ex-spouse probably will cross paths for some time to come, there is no better time than now to begin building an amiable relationship. This doesn't mean that you have to be good friends or get together socially, but it does mean that, where the children are concerned, you don't undermine one another.

But a qualifier is in order. There are many resources to help you to come to an understanding of your divorce and how you feel about your former spouse, and this book cannot address all the possible circumstances that lead to divorce and ill will between former partners. This belongs to the realm of postdivorce counseling and education. You need to grieve for your marriage just as you have for the loss of child custody. And you need support, information, and possibly professional counseling to deal with that grief. We'll be assuming here that some length of time has passed— that you've gotten beyond the stage where you are literally unable to be in the same room with your ex-spouse. If you're not there yet, don't despair; get help. Seek postdivorce counseling and keep gently working on your grief process.

You can also consult your attorney or inquire at your county courthouse about involving a mediator in your ongoing child custody arrangements to help facilitate otherwise impossible discussions and protect your rights. Many civil superior courts now offer this service, and in some states when custody and visitation are issues in a divorce, consultation with a family mediator is mandated. The court can either appoint a mediator, or you may choose a private family mediator who charges for services by the hour. Most private family mediators are also trained in various mental health fields.

Assuming, then, that there is communication between you and your ex-spouse, for your sake and the children's, you should try to keep that communication positive, especially when it comes to issues concerning the welfare of your kids. It's vital that you be able to speak civilly over the phone; that you pick up the children for visitations without getting in a jab or two at each other; that you agree on such issues as who'll attend parents' night at Johnny's school.

This was a goal Carole lost sight of in her quest to show her children how strong she was. A thirty-two-year-old computer analyst,

Carole was still insecure about whether twelve-year-old Sarah and ten-year-old Joshua still loved her after her custody loss. She felt compelled to prove to her children that she was the better parent. She made every effort to win the inevitable skirmishes she'd have with her ex-husband Alex when she picked up the children for their weekly visitation.

If Alex so much as reminded her of the kids' bedtime, she'd take offense and launch into a tirade, often when her children were present. "I thought he was trying to put me down in front of the kids," she recalled as she dug her fingernails into the arms of the chair in which she sat. "I remember thinking, 'That son-of-a-bitch! Here he'd won custody and now he was acting so pompous every time I picked up the kids—like I didn't know how to take care of them or something!' I thought I'd be damned if I was going to let him treat me that way in front of the children."

But after several months of this habitual arguing, Carole saw a difference in how her daughter and son responded to her. "Alex had even tried to explain that Sarah and Joshua were afraid of me coming to pick them up." Carole lit a cigarette and inhaled deeply before continuing. "Of course, I thought he was lying to make me look bad." She finally had to face the fact that something was wrong when, for the second weekend in a row, the children cried as they left with her Friday night and seemed relieved to return home to their father Sunday evening. Carole probed Sarah and Joshua about what they were feeling. Some of what she heard was painful, but it was unavoidably clear that the root of their anxiety was her front-porch battles with Alex.

Resolved never to fight again in front of her son and daughter, Carole began to make a point of handling her disagreements with Alex over the phone and out of the children's earshot. She said this new system for airing her grievances had two important advantages. First, Sarah and Joshua no longer balked when she picked them up and they all enjoyed happier, more satisfying weekends together. Second, Carole found that by the time she got a chance to call Alex with her complaints, her anger had often dissipated. The number of arguments dwindled dramatically, bringing some calm to an otherwise unpleasant situation.

Another reason to foster an amiable relationship with your former spouse is that you may reduce the likelihood that he or she will take you back to court. Many second-round court cases are born of an unresolved conflict between ex-spouses. One parent retaliates against the other by asking for more child support or a renegotiation of visitations. Investigations costing thousands of dollars can ensue, putting children and parents through question-and-answer sessions with social workers, lawyers and psychologists that leave emotional scars on everyone.

You may find yourself wondering, "Why must *I* be the one to smooth things over?" But without this effort, noncustodial parents especially may find that their relationship with their children is impaired. I've talked to many parents who, unable to cope with how irritated and uncomfortable they feel around their ex-spouses, begin to space their visitations with their children further and further apart. They "just can't stand" the smugness of an ex-spouse who was awarded primary physical custody of the children. Invariably when they do get into the same room with their ex-spouses, a hurtful shouting match follows and they then cannot fully enjoy their children's company during the visitation. After several of these fights, the custodial parent is alienated, and rarely takes the other parent's opinions into consideration.

Considering the Custodial Parent's Perspective

Let's try to tear down some of these barriers to communication. It may help you to think about the custody situation from the custodial parent's point of view.

While custodial parents are typically classified as the "winners" because they were awarded the children, parents with sole or primary custody sometimes feel they're the ones who received the raw deal in the custody settlement. While they're staying home with the kids, the noncustodial parent is finishing a college degree or advancing in a career. Parents with custody often see the other parent as spending money extravagantly while they remain on a discount-store budget. They also feel jealous that the parent without custody can date and travel "whenever they feel like it, while I'm tied to home with the kids." In addition, the other parent often complains that he or she is a full-time baby-sitting service for the noncustodial parent—"I'm raising his kids for him, and he gets all the fun on the weekends while I get the dirty clothes and homework end of it!" "Disneyland parents" in particular are targets for the other parent's jealousy since it's difficult to compete for popularity with the children when the "opposition" has more money and free time to shower on the kids.

Some of what can appear to be lack of consideration on the custodial parent's part may simply be ignorance or oversight. Parents who have custody sometimes fail to consult the other parent because it just doesn't occur to them to do so. This is especially true when visitation and phone calls are infrequent. "I try to keep my ex-spouse informed about all that goes on with Timmy," a custodial parent explains, "but we so rarely have time to talk that I sometimes forget to mention everything!" To the noncustodial parent who may be starved for news of and contact with the kids, the custodial parent's fairly reasonable explanation, "Oh, I forgot to tell you," is infuriating.

Custodial parents also mistrust the parent without custody when the kids consistently cry and act out following a visit. These behaviors are tiring, worrisome, and irritating to custodial parents who must iron them out long after the noncustodial parent is driving back home. They wonder, "What is my ex doing or saying to upset these kids so much?" and focus on you, the other parent, as the root of the children's difficulty in adjusting rather than on the situation as a whole.

In addition, custodial parents, like least-access parents, have their own emotional upheaval to deal with. They may still be in love with their former spouses; angry at the way the marriage ended; frightened that the noncustodial parents will kidnap the kids or begin another custody battle; intimidated by the impressive social and/or occupational positions the noncustodial parents hold. Custodial parents may secretly feel conflict over whether they really want custody and insecure about their parenting abilities. Custodial parents also feel that their every move as a parent is under a microscope, that the other parent is thinking, "Okay, you got custody, but when you slip up, I'll know about it."

So custodial parents are not always able to deal with circumstances at face value. For example, when a noncustodial parent says, "I'd sure like to have Donna for Christmas this year," the custodial parent may hear more than a simple request for holiday visitation. He or she may interpret the statement as, "I'd really like to outdo you by showering expensive toys on our daughter so that she'll want to live with me instead."

If you sense that your ex-spouse is unnecessarily threatened by you, address his or her fears and provide reassurance if appropriate. For example, if your ex-spouse expresses a far-fetched fear that you'll kidnap your daughter from school, you can allay this by talking about your respect for the law and the importance you place on your daughter's sense of stability. Say that your first priority is your daughter's physical and emotional health, and you would not do anything to jeopardize that, especially not ripping her away from her other parent without warning. Point out that the whole situation cannot work without *trust* between the two of you. Promise honestly to fulfill your end of the bargain and then follow that promise up behaviorally. (You can't do things that undermine your ex-spouse and then expect him or her to trust you.)

Following a messy divorce and custody suit, it may be easy to loathe your ex-spouse as an unfeeling being. But if you operate from this premise, you'll defeat yourself. You cannot create a positive environment for your children or a productive dialogue between you and your ex unless you honestly take into account how your ex feels. And yes, this makes for quite a paradox; when it comes to the kids, you need to learn to do something you may not have done when you were married—really listen to each other.

Problem Spots between You and Your Former Spouse

The feelings you hold toward your ex-spouse probably contain a mixture of endless possibilities. The emotions may be so tangled and mixed-up that a tremendous amount of effort will be required if they are to be sorted out, understood, and worked through. Much of this is part and parcel of the griefwork described in earlier chapters. Remember, as well, that the only person you can change is yourself. If, in counseling or on your own, you have realizations about the motives and behavior of your ex-spouse and yourself, those realizations can help you in your own healing process. And such realizations may also change the way you respond to your ex-spouse. But it is all too easy to use your feelings as a manipulative tool: "Well, I finally figured out why I hate your guts so much," or "I'm telling you how much you hurt me, so you have to be nice to me from now on."

Let's examine some of the most common emotions people cite when thinking of their ex-spouses. (Some suggestions for letting go of these feelings appear at the end of the chapter.) Which of these is creating conflict in your current relationship with your ex-spouse?

Anger and resentment. Those accusations and labels slung at you before the divorce or during the custody mediation may still ring in your ears every time your ex-spouse is around. You feel that some of the things your ex-spouse said and did are simply unforgivable. Instead of seeing another human, you see a compilation of all the past hurt and pain. You may engage in arguments for various reasons, ranging from wanting to beat the other person to the punch, to negative communication habits formed during the marriage, to plain old revenge.

Fear. While they are difficult emotions to admit to, everyone feels frightened, insecure and inadequate at times. Much of our fear has to do with power struggles that date back to childhood, when parents and teachers exercised control over our possessions and activities. This fear carries over to adulthood when we fear repercussions from powerful people (the boss who might fire you, the police officer who might arrest you).

Noncustodial parents may feel, consciously or unconsciously, that parents with custody have a greater amount of power. After all, they have the ability to withhold or interfere with visitation periods and contact with the children. Fear of emotional blackmail—"What will the kids hear about me?"—may also be involved. In addition, some custodial parents threaten lawsuits to increase child support as a means of controlling the behavior of the parent without custody.

Fear of your ex-spouse may be a remnant emotion, left over from a marriage rife with power struggles, physical abuse or emotional trauma. In some cases, the noncustodial parent may have surrendered the children in fear of an ex-spouse who seemed invincible.

Shame and guilt. Divorce and custody loss can lead to the feeling, "I failed. If only I'd been a (better, brighter, richer, more attractive, younger) person, this wouldn't have happened." Such thoughts and emotions can lead to a drop in self-confidence and self-esteem. If you are without custody, you very probably see the custodial parent as being "one up." After all, he or she *did* get custody.

With this mindset, it's easy to become intimidated by the other parent. Feeling inadequate in comparison to the parent who "won," you may even see yourself as a nobody, without the right to ask for anything. The custodial parent is likely to sense this impotency and take advantage of it. Certainly, the position of weakness won't command respect. But, while the noncustodial parent who feels like a failure may *expect* unfair treatment, it nonetheless will result in anger toward the parent with custody. We don't like to be mistreated, even when we believe it's deserved.

Guilt from having instigated the divorce either directly or indirectly can create huge barriers to communication. Every complaint the "instigator" presents is likely to be met with the reply, "Well, it's your fault; *I* didn't ask for the divorce!" A guilt-ridden parent may all too easily accept this answer.

Loneliness and unrequited love. Divorce usually leaves people feeling lonely and unloved. Custody loss, on top of it all, leaves many parents truly alone. The custodial parent, at least, has the company of the children and usually sympathetic support from friends and relatives. The noncustodial mother or father, by comparison, is often shunned or avoided by people with children that they used to socialize with or by friends who don't want to spend a lot of time with a depressed, grieving person. In addition, because the noncustodial parent usually moves out of the original house, he or she may also geographically separate from friends and relatives.

The parent without custody who craves adult interaction may react with desperation toward the other parent, inadvertently giving too much in an effort to gain acceptance from another person. Blunders that may occur when this happens include giving up some rights for visitation or agreeing to unrealistically high child support payments. In other words, the noncustodial parent becomes a "patsy." And this can happen the other way around. The custodial parent's social life may be severely cut back by being the sole caretaker of the children and he or she may court the favor of an ex-spouse who seems to have lots of friends and free time. Much of this has to do with the relationship dynamics that existed before the divorce; if your ex-spouse manipulated your feelings in a certain way when you were married—and/or *you* manipulated your spouse's—is this still going on?

Suppose one parent is still in love with the other and dreams of a reconciliation. How is this person going to react to any demands or requests that the other parent makes? Hoping for a re-established relationship, the still-in-love parent is likely to yield to any requests—fair or unfair—that the other parent makes.

Jealousy. Your ex-spouse left you for someone else. Or maybe you can't stand how happy and contented your ex-spouse seems to be now that you're divorced. These are common jealous reactions, but for parents without custody, the greatest and most overwhelming sense of jealousy comes from acknowledging what custodial parents have—time with the children. Time to watch them learn, laugh, grow, and play. Time to witness each of the numerous "firsts" that occur as a child grows up. Time to hear "Mommy!" or "Daddy!" called a thousand different ways.

The noncustodial parent's reaction is, "I'm jealous of what you have!"—a feeling that hurts in the pit of the stomach and in the heart. Any relationship contaminated with jealousy is strained at best because jealousy means competition geared toward gaining a limited, valuable goal—in this case, the children.

Relationships between noncustodial and custodial parents marred by the "green-eyed monster" are quite common. Although both parents are likely to be jealous of one another for quite different reasons ("You've got the kids!" "Oh yeah! Well, you've got the master's degree and the huge salary!"), it remains next to impossible to cooperate with anyone when competition exists between them.

In competitive situations, "winner" and "loser" are the roles assumed by contenders. One person will get the prize, and the other will return home with nothing. When custody battles place parents into adversarial positions with one another, they become enemies vying for the trophy of primary physical, or sole, custody. The winner/loser frame of mind that develops from custody contests often continues long after the court hearings are over. Let's look at how this situation can be turned around to allow both parties to win.

The Discussion Appointment: A Win/Win Approach

Visitation periods, in particular, are stressful for all concerned. Confronting an ex-spouse when picking up the kids for a weekend can be extremely uncomfortable and arguments may easily erupt. In addition to upsetting the children, such front-porch fights can set a negative tone for the entire visit.

It's important to learn how to refuse to be baited into an argument by your ex-spouse. People who have been married to each other know exactly what to say in order to push each other's "anger buttons." But once you identify something that really sets you off, the next time your ex-spouses tries to use it on you, your mindset changes a bit. Your reaction doesn't have to be automatic. Resolve *before* visitations that no matter what your ex-spouse says or does, you will not participate in making things worse by joining in the argument. It may help to imagine a wall between you and your ex-spouse, causing his or her words to bounce off you. Those words belong to him or her, not to you. If he or she becomes angry or resentful, that's unfortunate, but it's not your duty to resolve it. Your former husband or wife always has the option to discuss his or her concerns in a calm, adult manner.

When picking up the children for visitations, keep in mind the primary purpose of your being there: to transport the kids to be with you, so you can have a wonderful time with your children. Don't let anything ruin this.

If you and your ex-spouse have issues to discuss, make an appointment to talk about them at another time, so that the children aren't involved. If an argument or heated discussion is inevitable, take care of this at a time other than your visitation periods.

There will be disagreements with your ex-spouse, just because of the nature of the situation. Ironing out these differences requires great restraint to avoid resurrecting past hurts and side issues ("Well, I remember the time when *you* got drunk and slapped me!"). You may have spent a lot of time verbally sparring with one another before the divorce, and old habits are hard to break. A recent survey placed disagreements over childrearing practices as the number one reason couples argue. If the subject is that touchy during marriage, we can expect the situation to be even more volatile following divorce.

Discussion appointments, then, are mutually agreed-upon times when you and your ex-spouse sit down and talk about issues that surface about the children. You can encourage both compromise and agreement by pledging to yourself not to talk about irrelevant subjects. Stick to the topics that are of genuine concern such as Susie's math grades or Johnny's new baby-sitter. Write them down before the discussion appointment. Keeping the children safe from the negativity between the two of you should be at the top of your first agenda.

Among the ground rules of your appointment is that you meet at a place that is both out of the children's earshot and out of either parent's personal territory, such as office, home or "hang-out." For example, if Tony and Lisa were to meet at a restaurant next to Tony's office and all the waiters knew him on a first-name basis, Lisa might feel uncomfortable. Tony would have an edge in the negotiations, being more at ease in the surroundings and thus better able to concentrate on the issues at hand.

You should also hold the discussion appointment in a public place such as a restaurant. This will help you avoid the temptation to escalate into loud and unproductive name-calling sessions, and stick to rational discussions.

Each parent should bring a list of items to be covered and commit enough time to the appointment so no one feels cheated. Other ground rules for discussion appointments include:

—Both of you should take turns presenting an item for discussion.

—Refrain from accusations, foul language, hurtful words and raised voices.

—Avoid interrupting one another. If an idea or response pops up while your ex-spouse is talking, write it down and bring it up later.

—When agreements or compromises are reached, write them down so each will be clear on what is expected. This also avoids future arguments about "Well, you agreed to such-and-such before!"

—Avoid threatening one another ("I'll take you back to court!," "I'll leave with the kids!," etc.). Empty threats accomplish nothing and are barriers to agreements.

—If, after a particularly amiable discussion appointment, you're tempted to go home together for the night, think twice. If the children see you together, they may fantasize about a reconciliation and set themselves up for disappointment. You may also regret this temporary reunion if reconciliation is out of the question.

—Before ending the discussion appointment, set up a time and location for the next one. If you wait too long, you may be "stuffing" your anger until it explodes the next time you and your ex-spouse meet.

Debbie and Paul's first discussion appointment was a disaster. Both felt their egos were on the line. Both saw the appointment as a winner-takes-all situation. They ended up calling each other the hurtful names they used during their marriage and nothing was resolved. However, when Debbie consulted the counselor who had suggested the discussion appointment, she was able to see how rigid and defensive she had been with Paul. Reluctantly, Debbie swallowed her pride, called Paul and set up another meeting.

During the following appointment, Debbie forced herself to listen as her ex-husband shared his feelings. It was difficult, but she managed not to interrupt as he talked about their daughter, Jenny, and how he was concerned over her plunging grades and poor study habits. Paul afforded Debbie the same consideration as she talked about her fears that Paul would use Jenny's declining performance against her and thus further compound the guilt Debbie was already feeling about Jenny's difficulties. After an hour of give-and-take, the two were able to come to an agreement and mutually decided to arrange tutoring for Jenny.

One parent, determined to make the discussion appointment work, can influence the other by remaining calm and refraining from aggressive remarks. In time, the reluctant parent will realize that such meetings can be beneficial and represent perhaps the only way he or she can get a fair hearing.

Letting Go of the Past

There is a tendency, following divorce, to remember only the negative scenarios from a marriage—the bitter things said in anger, the extramarital affair, the overdrawn checking account. We refuse to allow ourselves to recall the picnics, warm hugs or surprise gifts. They make us feel vulnerable toward our ex-spouses. To remember the good is to open up our hearts and risk getting hurt all over again. So we develop selective amnesia.

After a bitter break-up, the loss of custody and a sizable child support order, noncustodial parents often wonder how they'll ever get along with the person who did all this to them—a person they can't even look at without getting angry.

Finding a solution involves letting go of the past. To some, the very thought of doing this will be threatening, because it will seem like forgiving the ex-spouse for the unforgivable. They ask themselves, "Why do I always have to be the one to give in? During our marriage I was constantly the one to make up and apologize first!"

However, letting go of the past does not mean caving in or accepting blame for something you didn't do. It is merely a way of putting the past into perspective so that it ceases, once and for all, to interfere with your happiness. When you don't recognize or understand old feelings, they will continue to control you in the present. If you try to ignore the past without first looking at it, you may keep acting in ways that don't make sense to you. Instead, feel the pain; remember the sadness. See the past for what it is, but then make the lifelong commitment to yourself not to sacrifice today for the sake of what you cannot change. If you feel your ex-spouse has taken a great deal away from you, if you keep trying to find a way to get even, he or she is still taking something from you every day.

"But," you may be saying, "I'm determined to forget the past, but my ex isn't! How can you have a logical discussion with someone who is absolutely determined to be irrational?" If you find that you constantly argue with your ex-spouse and cannot make a discussion appointment work, don't consider yourself a failure. There is plenty for you do to improve the situation on a daily basis, without the help of your ex-spouse: keep all arguments out of your children's sight and hearing; refuse to use the children as weapons *in any way*; use good judgment and common courtesy regarding when and how often you call or stop by the children's other residence; and keep to your own agreements, promises, and custody payment schedule.

Among couples who are willing to try it, many find postdivorce counseling helpful, or even necessary, in patching emotional wounds that get in the way of ongoing, effective parenting. The field of therapy for divorced couples is gaining popularity and more family counselors are offering this service.

In counseling, the estranged couple can work through disagreements with the therapist serving as an unbiased intermediary. When discussions begin to erupt into futile arguments, the counselor can intervene and guide the couple back to a productive and more relevant line of communication. Instead of bitterly dredging up the past, the two can focus on what's really bothering each of them today. When we're upset, we sometimes feel, "I have to be *right* first, then I'll be practical!" A counselor can point out this self-defeating behavior in each instance.

The goal of divorced parents is not to be in a state of ecstasy with one another, but to to communicate intelligently and trust that agreed-upon solutions will be carried out by both parties. You don't even necessarily have to *like* the other parent. You just need to have a cooperative relationship.

You might remember other people in your life—a boss, family member or teacher—whom you really didn't care for, but whom you still respected. Try to transfer that attitude to your ex-spouse and look objectively for his or her good points. Perhaps he or she is particularly good with the children or especially punctual and reliable about visitation periods.

Finally, a few words about forgiveness. The fact is that the resentment and anger you feel toward your ex-spouse don't hurt him or her nearly as much as they hurt you. You are the vessel which carries around these acidic emotions. Yet you may vow, "I'll never forgive!" Let's reframe the problem. Don't work on forgiveness: work on reducing your sense of the power that your ex-spouse has over you; work on letting go of negative feelings for your own sake.

Here are some thoughts, born out of my own and my clients' experiences, which may help. You can use them as daily affirmations or draw on them in tough situations:

—Every time I focus closely on my ex-spouse's behavior (with the exception of how the children are treated), I am allowing him or her to control my feelings, my thoughts, my life.

—I have the right to be angry at my ex-spouse. However, I am going to look at the anger, work through it, and let it go. I will not suffer from it any longer than is necessary.

—When I obsess about how badly my ex-spouse used to treat me, I am wasting more of my time on that person.

—Now that we're no longer married, my ex-spouse doesn't have any power over me. I simply need to respect his or her rights as outlined in the custody agreement.

—I don't need to get even with my ex-spouse, because it would serve no purpose. He or she probably wouldn't understand the "punishment." I would only be punishing myself.

—It doesn't matter whether my ex-spouse likes me or understands me deep down as a person. It does matter that *I* feel good about who I am and what I do.

—My ex-spouse's opinions of me are not definitive of me.

—I don't have to accept what, in my personal value system, is unacceptable in order to let go of the past.

—If I don't feel good about the way my ex-spouse treats my children and I am not able to work it out with him or her, there are legal means for me to protect them. I know my rights, I have personal power, and I will use it assertively.

In their book, *How to Forgive Your Ex-Husband and Get on with Your Life*, Marcia Hootman and Patt Perkins have the following to say about letting go of the past (it applies to both husbands and wives!):

> You can choose how long you wish to be stifled by your resentments. How long do you want to wait? . . . Give up the suppressed anger and resentment now. Look instead at the gifts your relationship brought you. Be grateful for the times you shared, the mutual friends you met and the children. Let go of the past so you can get on with the present . . . and the future—your future.

9

It's Not Just Your Custody Crisis: How Others Are Affected and Can Help

It's so hard never being able to see my grand-sons when I want to. I've never been one to be a complainer, so I hate to push my son all the time, but it's the only way I ever get to see them. Even then, I see them for only an hour or so every two months. If only it could be like it used to, and I could call or go over to see them whenever I wanted to. If only we could all be together at Thanksgivings and Christmases again.

> —Sixty-three-year-old woman whose son lost custody of her three grandsons a year and a half earlier

As Paul and his mother chatted over the phone one summer evening during their regular Sunday call, they reviewed the usual—how Uncle Timothy was doing, whether her gladioluses were in bloom, how Paul's work was going. Suddenly, she began to cry. "I haven't seen my grandkids since Easter and I'm so depressed," she sobbed. "Why did you and Joyce have to split up anyway?" During the rest of the conversation, Paul's mother described her insomnia and waning appetite in the six months since Joyce and their two daughters had left him. It wasn't the first time she'd poured out her sorrows. Virtually every weekend, she reminded Paul of how much she missed her granddaughters. He couldn't blame her, because he missed his little girls just as much. Once again, he listened patiently and did his best to comfort her, but for the rest of the evening, Paul couldn't shake off the guilt produced by that phone call.

Perhaps those most profoundly affected by the custody crisis, other than parents and children, are grandparents. Grandparents endure their own version of the custody crisis, with all its upsetting and mixed-up emotions. They experience shock, anger, panic, and depression in contemplating or experiencing drastically reduced contact with their grandchildren. They also may exhibit the same frantic denial and bargaining behaviors as their children, as they are forced to sit by and watch their grandchildren's fate being decided by others. They miss the shopping excursions for a grandson's birthday outfit and the cozy evenings spent cuddled together over a granddaughter's favorite book. They feel left out when friends swap "brag books" filled with current pictures of their grandchildren. They sigh when they realize how long it's been since they penciled in a grandchild's latest growth spurt on the height chart hanging from the kitchen wall. Most of all they feel powerless over when they'll see their grandchildren. Once a month? Once a year? Or ever again?

"Grandparents don't want a divorce from their grandkids!" cried Maria, a petite sixty-seven-year-old grandmother. Since Maria's son lost custody of his twin daughters five years earlier, she had seen the girls only three or four times per year compared to the every-weekend visits she was accustomed to before the divorce. She suspects her former daughter-in-law invents ways to make visits with Maria almost impossible. "I'm hurt because their mother doesn't understand that kids need to see both sets of grandparents," Maria said, becoming angrier and angrier as she talked.

"Right now, my mother is in the hospital dying of cancer," she sobbed. "I feel my grandkids should be able to see their great-grandmother before she goes."

The custody crisis is also hard for grandparents because they witness the anguish of their children and grandchildren. They listen to the accounts of court battles and watch previously stable children exhibit the mood swings, temper tantrums and deep depressions associated with divorce and custody split. It is incredibly painful for us to realize that "my divorce and custody battle are putting my parents through hell."

In addition, the role your parents play in your custody crisis can have a dramatic impact on how you handle it. They may be your staunchest allies during the custody battle—the ones most willing to listen quietly as you recount the latest struggle; the ones who'll help you pick up the pieces if custody is lost.

But your parents may intentionally or unintentionally add to your problems. Like Paul's mother, they may incessantly remind you of how much they miss their grandchildren. Others make their children feel guilty for getting divorced in the first place. Bob's father, for instance, confessed how disappointed he was with his son for getting a divorce, because he'd stayed with Bob's mother through some very bad times when he'd really wanted to leave. "The reason I didn't go was to give you and your sisters a decent life," he had said to Bob. Bob's father had felt a strong sense of duty toward preserving the family unit and resented Bob for what he referred to as his son's selfishness. This "I suffered, then so must you" syndrome adds one more layer to a divorced parent's sense of failure.

Many grandparents see their role in the custody battle as that of "coach." They cheer the parent every step of the way, lending support and advice. Unfortunately, some grandparents overstep their bounds and try to control every aspect of the court case, forcing the parent to ignore, forbid or dissuade them from further involvement in the custody fight.

The father of Rosalyn, my client, got quite involved in her custody case. He chose an attorney for her, paid her legal expenses and telephoned her constantly with his latest ideas on how to win the case. All of this was overwhelming to Rosalyn, first because she wasn't really sure whether she wanted custody, and because she was unused to getting so much attention from her father.

"I'm really caught in a bind," she said during one session. "On the one hand, I really appreciate my dad's help and all the attention's really nice too. How do I tell him to back off without hurting his feelings or seeming ungrateful? Or even worse, how do I get to have all the attention unless I let him control my custody case?"

In response to the trap in which she found herself, Rosalyn had become depressed and isolated. Her custody crisis had brought about something she really wanted—her father's animated interest in her. However, she was also mature enough not to like his butting in; she knew it was her life, not his. She said she knew she had to be honest with her father without making him feel foolish for his behavior. She badly wanted to tell him how much he meant to her and ask him to keep showing that he cared about her without trying to do things for her that she could do for herself. Rosalyn felt the best way to do this was by writing him a letter, so she could express everything she wanted to express without being overpowered by her father's objections.

We spent about two weeks working on a letter that Rosalyn felt good about giving to her father. Then she took him the letter and asked him to read it alone. The result was powerful. They ended up having a talk about how much they loved each other and needed to get closer, and how two adults can't have a truly close relationship when one is trying to dominate the other. (Rosalyn ended up negotiating a joint custody arrangement with her husband, and now each year her daughter spends six months with her ex-husband and six months with her.)

Harriet, another grandmother, offered to let her thirty-one-year-old son, Doug, move in with her following his separation from his wife and two children. She had no idea that she was about to experience the repercussions of Doug's custody crisis. Within two weeks after he moved in, Harriet sought counseling to deal with her frustrations over Doug's erratic temperament. "I'm ashamed to admit it," she cried, "but I can kind of understand why Gloria and the kids left him."

When Doug initially asked for his mother's comfort and advice, she gladly obliged. "The trouble was, I'd be right in the middle of telling him that he must be strong through this divorce and he'd start snapping my head off!" The two would then sulk the remainder of the evening. "He was so easy to talk to before," she complained.

She said she grew increasingly upset with Doug when she saw him cry over how much he missed his children. "My thinking that strong men don't cry didn't let me see the pain Doug was in. All I could feel was my own fear that I'd never see my grandkids again." Fearing she might lose the ability to see her grandchildren whenever she wanted, Harriet panicked when it seemed that Doug was caving in emotionally. "I wasn't aware of this, but I was scared that if Doug wasn't strong enough, he'd lose total custody of the kids," she explained. She'd startle Doug by barking orders for him to "stop crying this instant!" At the same time, he began to push Harriet away when she offered advice or tried to express her own feelings of grief. Doug and Harriet began to strike out at each other with increasing regularity.

It was at this point that Harriet came into therapy. One of the healing aspects of therapy is that you're able to voice your deepest feelings to another person—the therapist—and then watch how that person reacts. In doing this, you learn that it's okay to have conflicting feelings. Harriet realized it wasn't weird or crazy to truly want to comfort her son and, at the same time, be terrified that he would become emotional and helpless at the crucial moment in court, and then she'd lose all contact with her grandchildren. Therapy provided a safe testing ground for Harriet to try out how it felt to be completely honest with another person.

When she was finally able to put all of her feelings on the table, so to speak, Doug, in turn, expressed some of his fears to his mother. It was the beginning, after thirty-one years, of an honest relationship between mother and son.

Talking It Out with Your Parents

It is painful to listen to your parents cry over your custody loss. And, especially in families unaccustomed to talking about feelings, it's hard to know where to begin to talk with them. But unfortunately, your pain and your parents' pain, when left unexpressed, can build a wall between you.

The custody crisis can mark a turning point in your relationship with your parents. It can be the time for you to shed the juvenile-to-adult way you may still relate to your parents. It's the time to openly and honestly talk about how you—as a separate, mature adult—feel. Next time your parents say something about their hurt, anger, resentment, pain, or even ambivalence about your custody situation, seize the opportunity to have a more in-depth discussion about your feelings and their feelings. Here are some examples of what you might say:

—I know you miss the children, really I do. I miss them so much sometimes I can't stop crying.

—The divorce/custody arrangements can't be blamed on any one person, point in time, or incident. There were many circumstances and factors, and I want to tell you what I think those are. I want us to discuss it. But I also want you to know that over these last few months I've come to feel it's a mistake and it's harmful to blame anyone or use oversimplified excuses.

—You seem to be really angry, and I wonder if there's something you want to tell me. I'd really appreciate it if you'd tell me about it directly so we can talk about it. (Note: Although it feels frightening to say this, it really works!)

—I really care about your feelings about my custody situation. But sometimes I feel so guilty about the whole thing that it's hard for me to see your pain. It makes me feel that I'm responsible for the whole thing, when my head tells me that (name of ex-spouse) is also responsible.

Say what is true for you at the moment. Whatever it is, it's okay as long as you're not saying it manipulatively—to elicit some specific response from your parents. It's normal for your relationships with others to change, grow, and mature over time. And the same is true for your relationship with your mother and father. Being honest with one another and comforting one another brings you together and helps heal the wounds. In addition, you may recommend that your parents talk with a counselor if their grieving seems severe.

Also consider that your parents may be blaming themselves to some degree for your custody loss: if only they'd done something differently, helped you more, etc., you wouldn't have lost custody. Or maybe they regret that they divorced when you were young. In short, your parents may be more concerned with their own issues of guilt and self-blame than with how you feel about what's happened in your life. They may snap at you and say things they'll later regret, mostly because of the stormy clash of feelings going on within them. If you sense this, you need to get these issues out into the open.

Finally, if you have lost your parents, or are not close to them (and it doesn't look like this crisis is going to bring you any closer), remember that there are many other sources of constructive support available to you. Close friends, other family members, parent support groups, professional counselors, and clergypeople can all serve as faithful allies. Don't try to go it alone!

Talking to Friends and Coming out of the Custody Closet

After his divorce, Tom realized something that surprised and saddened him: his ex-wife had been the only person with whom he had ever shared his feelings. Without her, he had no one to talk to.

"One day I mentioned to a co-worker that I wouldn't be working that weekend because it was my turn to have the kids,"

Tom recalled. "He hadn't even realized that I'd recently gone through a divorce and had lost custody. He told me he was in the same boat and so were a lot of other guys at work." Through this co-worker, Tom met a whole network of fathers without custody. "It was almost an underground club with the common element that we all missed our kids. I couldn't believe it! Managers, engineers and mechanics—they all gave me the support I needed."

As noncustodial parents, we face the question of whether and in what way to share our pain with friends. When talking to friends about your custody situation, it's best to be straightforward and honest. For example, you might simply say something like, "Yes, the last six months have been very rough." Let a short answer show how you feel without launching into all the intimate and painful details. This will keep you connected to friends who are important to you, but who you feel are not willing or able to be there for you for long periods of time. In other words, don't think your only options are tortured silence or pouring out the whole saga.

During my first three years without custody, I lived in the "custody closet." I spent a lot of energy concealing my custody loss and the fact that I had children. If someone asked whether I had kids, I'd mumble something about, "not yet" (justifying this lie with the underlying half-truth that the kids were "not yet" at my house). Or, I'd say my second husband Dwight and I were waiting to have children (another half-truth—my husband and I have thought about having children in the future).

I never intended to con or hurt anyone. I was simply trying to spare myself the pain of having one more person insinuate I was any less a mother for not having custody of my children. As a result, I became an expert at steering conversations away from the subject of children. I asked long-time friends not to tell new acquaintances about my children, putting photos of the kids away when company came over and trying not to reveal much knowledge of childbirth, diapering or booster-shots.

Gradually, like most secrets, mine grew enormous and distorted until it seemed that the truth I harbored was akin to having murdered someone. Looking back, I'm embarrassed for having blown everything out of proportion. But I know that when I was going through my secrecy phase, I was dealing with my pain the best way I knew. It was a coping skill, developed out of my circumstances and a poor self-image.

Friendship with just one nonjudgmental, caring person helps us safely release anger and bitterness, sort out real feelings from other people's standards, and, yes, see the positives and even the humor in our situations. When I finally burst my bubble of silence, I did so guided gently by another noncustodial woman. She was my boss at a hospital where I was a counselor. I knew she had been without her son and daughter for several years, but I initially felt like no one, not even another noncustodial mom, would understand.

About a year after I'd begun working for her, the frequency of my visitations with Chuck and Grant was finally increased at my request. Since they lived three hours from me, it took a whole day of driving to pick the boys up and bring them to my house. I began to ask for a lot of time off work without telling my boss why. Coincidentally, she was also periodically taking time off from work to travel to see her own kids. Still, I felt different and afraid.

After asking for a day off for the fifth week in a row, I began to feel frightened that my job would soon be in jeopardy. It became clear that I had no choice but to confide in her. Any excuse I could have come up with would have seemed trite compared to missing work for the sake of my children.

Once I opened up to my boss, she helped me see that by keeping my children a secret, I was depriving others of getting to know a special dimension of myself. In fact, she thought more highly of me because I was a mother, whether my two boys lived with me or not. She helped me unveil my parenthood by teaching me to love that part of myself again. Everyone needs nurturing guidance such as this and I only wish that it hadn't taken me three years to meet her.

Perry's experience also nicely illustrates the importance of friends. His wife had left him, taking their two sons with her. When Perry decided to initiate a custody suit, his co-workers and relatives scoffed. "They thought I was trying to get out of paying child support," Perry said, slowly shaking his head. Their lack of support made him feel alone and insecure about the legal battle ahead of him. He also became extremely depressed. "At that time," Perry remembered, "I almost gave up on people."

Although Perry felt that everyone was against his attempts to win custody, two friends, David and Steve, did come over to visit and console him. David had lost custody of his own children two years before, and Steve could also sympathize with Perry, because

Steve's parents had divorced when he was quite young. "Those guys came over almost every night and really helped me to feel better about what I was doing," Perry recalled with a broad smile. That first visit and subsequent ones from his friends marked the turning point of his custody crisis.

While a good friend will be glad to listen, he or she may eventually avoid you if all you can bring to the relationship is an onslaught of self-pity. The resulting loneliness will increase your feelings of guilt, depression, and probably embarrassment. You'll be sitting alone at a time when you most need to take the focus off feeling sorry for yourself.

What this really means is that during your custody crisis, as at all times, the key to maintaining high quality friendships is being a good listener. Sometimes in the long process of grieving, about all you can manage is to let out what you feel inside. But another valuable way to heal is through establishing an intimate give-and-take connection with someone else. Everybody has problems, and everyone is, in different ways, vulnerable. We gain immeasurable wisdom, insight, and comfort in sharing other people's burdens. Helping others is helping ourselves. So, give your friends the undivided attention you need in return from them. Remember that when you're hurting, you are not looking so much for advice as you are for a sympathetic hearing and support. A good listener provides just that. He or she listens, nods, asks for clarification, reiterates, and doesn't interject opinions and beliefs that aren't relevant to the speaker's feelings. Nor does a good listener try to talk the speaker out of his or her feelings (though sometimes it's tempting.)

If you feel you don't have friends to do this process with, please see chapter 11 and the information on support groups for noncustodial parents that is provided at the end of the book. You are *not* alone.

In teaching children how to approach an essay without apprehension, teachers remind kids of the expression, "I don't know what I think until I see what I say." You, too, may not know what you feel until you see what you say. Another friend who can help you see what you're saying is you, yourself. I highly recommend the proven practice of keeping a "feelings journal." This can be a bound journal or diary, a pad of paper, or whatever's handy to write on at the time. Don't worry about dating the entries, style, grammar or whether you should or shouldn't feel what you're saying you feel.

Don't think you have to write something every day. When you have an important thought about your custody crisis, or get in touch with a general feeling, a belief, or a raw emotion that you think is significant, write it down. It might help to note the circumstances under which this happened, and perhaps how your body feels or felt. A recent study showed that writing your feelings is almost as effective as psychotherapy in helping to sort through and release confusing feelings.

Keep something to write on handy all the time and jot down what's inside you and true for you at the moment. If privacy's a concern, you can tear the paper up afterwards. Some people do, however, find it interesting to go back and read their journals. You may see patterns, and, importantly, you can see progress toward healing and peace.

Dealing with the Negative Reactions of Others

While your parents, relatives, and close friends may share the biting pain of your custody loss, others may react differently. Acquaintances, neighbors, co-workers and even the person who cuts your hair may all seem to have opinions about your custody status.

Four months after I separated from my husband and children, I was at a new job in a new city. Feeling a need to share my pain, I reluctantly opened up to my co-workers about my noncustodial status, knowing they had no prior experience with a mother without custody. Although they didn't offer their opinions to me directly, I did find out a lot about the eldest woman's feelings on another occasion when I mentioned that I was attending college after work. "Well, I certainly wouldn't leave my children," she said emphatically.

Her statement hit me very hard. It triggered my own conflicts about right and wrong. But instead of talking to her, I remained silent—for three years. The combination of my low self-esteem, my suspicion that I *was* a terrible person for being without my children (and enjoying myself at times) and my co-worker's remark made me throw a cloak of secrecy around my children. I left that job, and I didn't tell anyone that I had children or had even been married before, until I opened up to that special boss three years later.

Parents without custody often feel no one understands the very unique pain they endure. When otherwise well-meaning individuals ask me what I did that was so wrong as to cause me to lose custody,

I still cringe in disbelief. In chapter 11, we'll discuss the particular prejudices that women face and those that men face. However, there are several measures we all can take to protect ourselves from the ignorant or insensitive remarks of others.

First, when people make "offhand" but cutting statements or implications about your custody situation, immediately but very politely ask them to clarify what they meant. In doing so, you assert your sense of self—you communicate that, although you definitely don't want to become combative or misunderstand, neither will you listen to an unkindness or untruth about yourself without pointing out that it is unkind or untrue. Take some time to think up a couple of noncombative, assertive responses that would work for you. If assertiveness is a particular problem for you, practice saying them in the mirror.

When people query you directly about why you lost custody, simply ask why they want to know. Many people will retreat realizing your custody status is none of their business. I think you'll find that some people may simply want to know you better. Or perhaps they're grappling with their own custody crisis. Should you choose to explain your situation—and remember, that is your right—you and that person could end up forming a mutually beneficial alliance.

It's also important to recognize that others are uncomfortable and unsure of what to say. Just as we are often at a loss for words around someone who has recently lost a family member (is "I'm sorry" enough or appropriate?), some people feel awkward about what to say to someone who is apart from his or her children. Even with the divorce rate as high as it is today, lost custody or split custody doesn't seem to fit into a tidy niche, and others may feel uncomfortable dealing with it. Many have never known a woman without custody or a man fighting to regain it. They may be uncertain about whether to express sympathy or congratulations when they're unsure about your feelings surrounding your custody arrangements. Help them by indicating how you do feel about your custodial status. You can guide the reactions of friends, relatives and co-workers through your nondefensive, general explanation of what the custody arrangement is and a brief, calm expression of how you feel about it—"No, I'm not happy about it, but my lawyer and I are dealing with it" or "It's the best for all concerned at this point."

Also remember your right to say as little as you want to. If you feel uncomfortable discussing your custody situation, that's justification enough for steering the conversation away from the subject.

In addition, you don't have to justify the reasons for your custody situation to anyone. If others pressure you for information or an explanation, don't give in. You have the right to pick and choose what you want to disclose to others, regardless of the arguments they present. You also don't need others' approval about your custody status. After all, it's how *you* feel about the situation that is most important.

You've been working on listening to and trusting your feelings. Use that skill in dealing with inquisitive people. Don't feel compelled to fill in the missing pieces for people if your gut-level feeling about them is that they're untrustworthy. You may not want to say anything more than, "I have two children, a boy and a girl." Part of taking care of yourself means reserving personal information for those people you trust. Period.

After I finally came out of the custody closet, quite a few of my co-workers wanted to know all about how I'd lost custody in the first place. Sometimes I felt their motive was more to be entertained than to know me better. In that case I'd usually say, "You know, I don't talk about my custody loss because I've found that some people actually imply that I don't love my children or that I didn't want them. And that hurts so much that it's easier not to discuss it in the first place." Often the person I was talking to would not want to be anything like THOSE PEOPLE who'd misjudged me, so he or she would be a bit more careful when discussing my custody loss in my presence or out of my earshot.

Finally, try to be aware of how people react to bad news. It's human nature to believe that life is fair, an assumption that social psychologists call the "just world syndrome." This type of thinking leads people to believe that awful, horrible things could only happen to people who deserved them, "not to people like me." By blaming the victim, they feel personally invulnerable to tragedy. They want to believe that if they are well-behaved and careful, nothing bad will ever happen to them.

It thus follows that others will blame noncustodial parents for doing something out of the ordinary to cause their custody loss. Women who lose custody will be labeled unfit and men without custody may be explained as "guys who haven't sown their wild oats," or worse, fathers who abandoned their families. These labels serve to organize otherwise senseless information and help calm fears that good, decent everyday folks don't lose custody of their children. But then you know only too well that this isn't true.

10

When Thoughts of Regaining Custody Rage Inside You

*The pressure of deciding what to do—should I
go back to court and try to get custody or
not?—is really eating at me. It seems like I
can't mention missing my kids without
whoever I'm talking to trying to pressure me
into a custody suit. And I don't know whether
I'm ready or not. But in the meantime, the
clock is ticking and I know that the longer you
wait, the harder it is to get custody back.*
　　　　　—Twenty-nine-year-old parent
　　　　　　　without custody, two years
　　　　　　　following custody loss

If your ex-spouse has primary physical custody of your children, it's
bound to happen to you sometime. Maybe it will be triggered by
your child whimpering, "I don't want to leave!" at the end of a
visit. Or perhaps it will simmer through several clashes over child
support with your ex-spouse. Maybe you gave up custody voluntarily
but now find yourself in a much better position, financially and/or
emotionally, to raise your kids. Eventually, the question surfaces:
"Should I try to get my children back?"

Usually, this internal struggle is based on unknowns: What
would it be like to return to court and what are the possible
outcomes? Could you endure losing custody again? How would you
know which attorney to hire? Could you potentially end up in a
worse situation with decreased visitation and increased child support?
What will the cost be in terms of money, time and emotions? Will

you under- or overestimate those commitments? More importantly, what are your true motives for wanting to return to custody court?

Many noncustodial parents find that after several months or years of hearing others ask, "Why don't you go back to court and get custody?," it's difficult to remember whose idea the thought of regaining custody was. If you let others push you into regaining custody when you're not ready, the results for your children and for you can be quite damaging. And if you lose, without having prepared for that possibility, the grief can be overwhelming.

Your Child's Role in the Decision

Parents naturally want to please their children, so when a little voice pleads at the end of a visitation, "Please, can't I live with you?" it's tough not to consider another custody suit. Children frequently are the motivating factor in second-round custody trials.

However, your children may lack the judgment and foresight necessary to determine what's best for them. It's up to you to learn your children's motives for wanting to live with you.

Do they have the impression that life with you will be one extended, happy vacation? Often, children associate life with the custodial parent with drudgery while they think of life with the noncustodial parent as a recurring round of fun, presents, ice cream, and movies. They need to understand that, if they ever were to live with you, they would most likely have the homework, chores and bedtimes they have now.

Are they saying they want to live with you to express how much they care about you? To children, saying "I want to live with you" to a parent can be the ultimate way of conveying, "I love you." In other words, your child may not mean she literally wants to live with you. She could just be trying to tell you that she cares a great deal about you and will miss you very much until she sees you again.

Are there other possible motives your child could have for wanting to live with you? Is he looking for escape from a class that he's failing at school? Expressing a desire to live with you may be your child's way of signaling that something is bothering him or something is lacking in his life; it may be a "the grass is always greener" situation. Your child may think, "If I lived with Mom (or Dad), I'd have more friends and be more popular," or, "my teachers would like me." If you think this is the case, encourage your child to talk about why he doesn't feel good about himself and consider some short-term counseling. Help him explore ways to meet people and get involved in activities in his current school or neighborhood.

Are you rewarding your children in some way for asking to live with you? Children are quick to discover what pleases their parents. Recall how you responded to your child the last time she said she wanted to live with you. Chances are you smiled and hugged her warmly. Such attention encourages children to repeat the same thing again without necessarily meaning exactly what they say.

Are your children making serious allegations about the quality of care at their primary home? Such accusations can range from complaints about psychological abuse such as being ignored or constantly belittled to physical abuse involving slapping, shaking or not being given enough to eat.

Occasionally, these charges can be a child's way of retaliating against a parent for not allowing a date to go past midnight or refusing to buy a new bicycle and so forth. Again, this is especially true if you reward your child for telling you things about your ex-spouse. However, any hint of abuse should be taken seriously and investigated.

If the child has any marks or scars, or is telling you stories about past serious injuries such as broken bones or gashes, consult a physician immediately. A medical doctor can determine if physical abuse has occurred and to what extent. Like a psychotherapist, the doctor is bound by law to file a child abuse report in the case of suspected mistreatment. If physical abuse is present, obviously this throws the "should I or shouldn't I sue for custody" question into a very different light. Consult your attorney about what options you have to protect the child at the present time as well as the legal implications.

Psychological abuse, on the other hand, is a vast gray area. However, a child who is being verbally mistreated or neglected will reflect the consequences over time, exhibiting behavioral or emotional problems such as stealing, dwindling school performance and lying. If you are concerned, consult a psychotherapist and again, talk to your attorney about the ramifications. Many parents have restraining orders enacted to protect their children from specific behaviors by their ex-spouses which can be spelled out in the order, such as "no verbal abuse," or, "no corporal punishment."

Some Reasons of Your Own

Certainly, the thought of regaining custody may occur to you even if your children haven't suggested it or are well-treated by your ex-spouse, but it's very difficult to untangle your motives. It may help to look over the various reasons commonly cited by parents thinking about returning to court. Examine your thoughts and feelings about each one.

You may have serious philosophical differences with your ex-spouse about the children's upbringing. Maybe you don't belong to the religion your child is being brought up in or perhaps you don't think the other parent takes a strong enough stand in favor of higher education. Maybe you don't like the school the custodial parent has selected. Or you feel the kids are growing up in an unsavory neighborhood. Perhaps your objections revolve around your ex-spouse's dating habits, choice of friends or the number of hours he or she works.

Parents who consider initiating a custody suit because they have such lifestyle objections should first ask themselves, "Could I solve my differences with my ex-spouse's parenting style through other means?" Maybe postdivorce counseling or just sitting down and talking can result in compromises or positive changes. In other words, try not to view a return to court as the only solution.

You may want to spend more time with your children. This is perfectly understandable, given how quickly little Johnny progresses from taking his first step to asking for your car keys. You may panic that you've already missed out on too much of your child's life and decide to dive into another custody case "before any more time is wasted."

Your desire to spend more time with your children isn't unreasonable and could be satisfied through means other than the courtroom. First, approach your children to see how they feel about spending more time with you. Then talk to your ex-spouse about it. A discussion appointment (chapter 9) is an ideal time to bring up your wish for increased visitations. If visitation, and not custody, is the primary reason you're unhappy with your situation, explore with your lawyer the possibility of going back to court for increased visitation rights.

You may believe that custody will turn your unhappy life around.
Are you plagued by feelings of emptiness and dissatisfaction? Do
you avoid being alone at all costs? If so, you may begin to feel that
the only way to fill the void in your life is to regain custody of your
children. But there's a big difference between feeling you'd be
happier having custody and the haunting awareness that "I'm
miserable inside and need something or somebody to fix it for me."
Release from such feelings must come through introspection,
preferably with a skilled counselor.

*You may feel that fighting for custody will show your children how
much you love them.* "How will my children know that I love them
unless I continue to fight for custody?" This prevalent fear among
noncustodial parents can have many sources, ranging from the
insecurity of feeling out of touch with a child, to pressure from
others who make you feel guilty about your noncustodial status.
Have you made a strong and continual effort to have quality time
with your children? Have you worked with them to keep open the
lines of communication and let them know that you are there for
them at all times? You don't have to have custody of your children
to show them that you love them unconditionally.

You may be tired of the inconveniences of your noncustodial status.
You're fed up with paying child support. The quick turn-around of
weekend visitations is exhausting you. You've tried unsuccessfully for
five nights straight to reach your kids on the telephone. You're
beginning to fantasize about how nice it would be to put the burden
of being the part-time parent on your ex-spouse. If this describes
you, take a look at your lifestyle—is it unbalanced? Do you regularly
draw from your "well" of giving, helping, solving, fixing, working
and planning, without replenishing your serenity with a few minutes
a day of self-care, meditation, and receiving care from others? Could
the cause of your weariness be burn-out in other areas of your life—
your financial situation, your overextended work schedule, your
overdue term paper? Having custody of the kids won't lessen these
stresses. It could, instead, add to them.

*You may want to escape the social stigma of being a parent without
custody.* Noncustodial women, in particular, may want to avoid the
negative stereotypes of their noncustodial status more than they want
custody of their children. Fathers without custody may be under

pressure to do what all "the other dads" seem to be doing, namely, seeking custody.

You may secretly want revenge against your ex-spouse. Perhaps the most destructive of all motivations for renewing a custody case, this reaction is an outgrowth of the adversarial winner/loser set-up of most divorces and custody disputes. It's difficult to shake this orientation even long after the custody settlement. Nobody wants to be viewed as a loser, and this can fuel the desire to ask for a rematch to regain the "championship title."

After having relinquished custody of their two children two years before, Sandy learned that her ex-husband, George, had recently been dating her best friend. Sandy was deeply hurt and interpreted their actions as a personal assault, and indeed, perhaps it was. The only thing she could think of to redress the situation was to threaten to take custody back. Both parents spent thousands of dollars in legal fees and waged a bitter war, and in the end Sandy won custody and a hefty child support award.

Sandy soon discovered, however, that her original reasons for surrendering custody—she disliked being responsible for other people and didn't cope well with others being dependent on her—were unchanged. She simply had wanted to punish George. So, just three months after winning custody, Sandy returned the children to him. By this point, George had suffered through loss of sleep, time off work and a substantial debt resulting from court costs. But most significantly, their children had suffered incalculably. They had felt secure with their dad, but now worried that they could be forcibly transplanted to their mom's residence at any time.

You may be pressured by someone else to fight for custody. Your parents, other relatives, minister, boyfriend, girlfriend or new spouse probably have their own reasons for wanting you to have custody. But you are ultimately the one who will bear the cost of and stress of the custody suit. Furthermore, you're the one who will feel the enormous impact of life as a custodial parent.

Once you've clarified the various reasons that led you to think about changing your custody status, it's time to think about the relative validity of each. Consider and reconsider your answers to these questions and each time, write down your answers.

—Why do I want custody?

—What would my life be like if the children were living with me full-time?

—Would I be happy?

—Would the children be happy?

—What changes in my lifestyle would I have to make if I were awarded custody? How would my job change? Would some of my career goals be jeopardized? How would my social life change?

—Am I willing to make those changes?

In regard to the custody trial, ask yourself the following:

—Can I withstand months of courtroom appearances, investigations and personal questions? Can I deal with the stress in a healthy manner?

—Can I financially afford the cost of a custody case or will someone have to help me?

—Am I able to take the necessary time off work to go to court and to meet with the investigators?

It's very hard to look at underlying, and possibly unhealthy reasons for wanting custody. We all like to believe that, when it comes to our children, we never think of ourselves first. That's why it's also hard to look at the fears that are holding us back from a custody suit. Realistically, the prospects of getting back into a courtroom battle are frightening. In addition to fears about the expense and time involved, the frustrations of dealing with judicial red tape and the potential for being humiliated by your ex-spouse's attorney, if you lost, would you have the strength to pick up the pieces of your life all over again?

Some parents' fears are even longer range. They worry what life would be like if they won custody. After life as a noncustodial parent, many mothers and fathers enjoy a flexible schedule, free of encumbrances and time constraints. Of course, they love their kids and would like to spend more time with them—but live with them full-time after enjoying all that free time? Be honest: no matter how much you want your kids, that's a big change.

Reluctance to return to court doesn't reflect whether you're a good mother or father. Instead, it indicates that you're just not ready to seek custody; that it would not be good for your children or for you to seek custody; that it would not be good for your children or for you if you were to regain custody. A good parent very carefully and honestly weighs motives, fears, and hopes before making this decision.

Making Decisions

If it's been several months, maybe years, since your custody loss and yet you continue to obsess over the question, "Should I go back to court or shouldn't I?," perhaps this indecision is a way of avoiding having to answer yes or no once and for all. The longer you can postpone a final decision about whether to return to court, the longer you can avoid fully accepting custody loss. You can fool yourself indefinitely into thinking your custody loss is only temporary by saying, "I'm going to sue for custody when . . . ."

For those parents who are undecided and who feel as yet unprepared to decide, the best decision is to decide not to decide. Release yourself from an "I have to say yes or no" stance. If people ask you, inform them, "I don't know what I'm going to do about custody right now, and at this time I'm not prepared to make a decision." This will help disentangle your private reflections from other people's motives and standards and from your own "I shoulds."

Bert, a thirty-year-old construction worker, was a newly-recovering alcoholic and father without custody for nearly four years when he began to reassess his life. During this period of introspection, he realized how much his two sons meant to him. He seriously considered going to court to try to get the boys from his ex-wife's parents who'd been awarded custody. But his therapist warned, "A newly sober person is fragile that first year." Without his newfound sobriety, he was no sort of father to his sons. He decided to concentrate on maintaining his sobriety and on being a good father to his sons even though they didn't live with him. Such a decision is not irrevocable, but it is a smart way to reduce daily stress.

Jeannie, a twenty-seven-year-old receptionist who came to me for therapy, related the way her decision not to sue was made. She had been a mother without custody for almost two years before she began to think about trying to regain custody of her son. The first thing she did was contact a lawyer to see what her chances would be. She was prepared for some pretty depressing statistics, but none as bleak as the ones she heard. Her lawyer said that unless Jeannie could prove her ex-husband unfit, the courts were against changing the child's residence in most cases. He then explained some of the cumbersome procedures involved in custody cases and how much time and money she could expect to invest.

Jeannie was nearly in tears by the time the attorney got around to discussing his $1,500 retainer fee, the costs of mandatory court-ordered psychological examinations on herself, her ex-husband and her son, and the amount of time she could expect to be off work for court appearances and meetings with social workers. She couldn't believe that even after all the time and money that would be involved, the odds of her regaining custody were still slim. Discouraged but not yet defeated, Jeannie consulted another lawyer. He confirmed what the other attorney had told her.

For the next two nights, Jeannie lay awake sorting through her options but continually confronting the same financial obstacles. She didn't have enough money for the attorney's retainer fee, let alone other court costs. She also feared that by taking too much time off work, she'd risk losing her new job. Finally, Jeannie had to face the fact that financial constraints had made her decision for her. This is probably the single biggest reason why parents decide against another suit.

When you come to a negative decision, you may feel intensely guilty. If you've gotten your own parents' hopes up by mentioning the possibility of going back to court, now it seems you've let them down again. You have to endure that painful twinge when your child asks, "Don't you ever want me to live with you again?" You become enmeshed in regrets that begin with "if only . . . ." You say to yourself, "If I were really a good parent, *nothing* would stop me from getting custody back."

Parents who take the decision-making process very seriously, and go about it in a thorough, business-like manner are less likely to be hard on themselves later. This means you should: talk to others who have returned to the courtroom and gather both the facts and a sense of the emotional process involved; interview at least two attorneys about your particular case; read relevant newspaper and magazine articles; attend noncustodial parents' support group meetings; and most importantly, talk to yourself at length. Only you know what you truly feel, think and want. Only you know what you can and cannot adjust to. Only you know what your financial situation is.

If you spend a lot of time—on the order of several months—thinking about it and doing research and decide against another custody suit at this time, that should be that. At that point, deliberately decide to stop torturing yourself with needless guilt or anger over the decision. Practice the affirmations you have created for yourself. Focus on the here and now in your relationship with your children.

Custody and Your New Spouse

Although this is the noncustodial parent's decision, and no one should pressure him or her into it, by the time they consider returning to court, many noncustodial parents are remarried. If you have remarried, another person will be profoundly affected by your quest for custody. Be sure that a custody suit is something you both want.

If your new spouse is also a noncustodial parent, consider whether there will be resentment if you don't try to regain custody of his or her children as well. If your new husband or wife doesn't have kids, it's especially important to explore his or her feelings about being thrust into the role of full-time stepparent. Your new spouse may resent the loss of freedom that comes with the responsibility of raising children. He or she may have nagging doubts about whether he or she has the parenting skills necessary to cope when your child gets into trouble or asks for guidance. You also need to make certain your spouse likes your children and that he or she isn't simply going along with your custody battle to please you.

Lexi is a thirty-one-year-old full-time stepmother. She admitted it hasn't been easy over the past two years since they assumed custody of her husband's two daughters at the request of his ex-wife. Lexi described the idyllic life she and Gordon led during the first year they were married: they had plenty of time for weekend get-aways and jogging along the boardwalk in front of their small beachfront home. But when they agreed to assume custody, Gordon and Lexi gave up their house and moved to the suburbs so the girls, aged eight and fourteen, wouldn't have to leave their school and friends. "They're wonderful kids but they expect their dinner on the table at six o'clock, refuse to clean their rooms and argue all the time—the typical things kids do. I'm just not sure I was prepared for all this," said Lexi, who'd never been married before. She added that she takes pride in the fact that she and Gordon have provided the girls a stable, nurturing environment. But the overwhelming responsibility of raising two daughters has caused her to have second thoughts about whether she and Gordon should have a baby of their own. "Sometimes," she said with a tired but good-natured giggle, "I tell Gordon that when I saw him coming up to me at the party where we met, I should have run the other way."

It's a good idea to discuss, up front, the strain which fighting for custody may put on your new marriage. Make your new spouse aware of the time and expense involved as well as the stress of long-term uncertainties over "will or won't we win?" He or she should also anticipate last-minute changes in court dates or the seemingly unnecessary days spent before a judge only to have the really important decisions delayed over and over. And expect that through all this, the bills will mount.

Your new marriage partner should also be aware of how very unpleasant custody cases can be. He or she should be prepared for the intense scrutiny you may both undergo in regard to your parenting skills, character strength and morality. You'll be in a position to help your new spouse to resist taking personally any mudslinging that may result. For instance, accusations of abuse are often made against stepparents. Your spouse should also be ready for interviews with social workers and possibly, psychological testing. All these things—all the negatives—should be discussed beforehand, and you should also carefully review all the positives: "This is important and worthwhile for us to pursue because . . . ." These positives will be the things you draw on and remind one another of in times of stress.

Because of his or her role in the new custody battle, your spouse may be intensely afraid of "blowing it" and losing the entire case. Knowing how important the custody battle is to you, your spouse may worry, "You'll never forgive me if I do something that causes us to lose!"

Each of you will need a tremendous amount of emotional support at a tumultuous time when neither may be capable of giving it. For this reason, anything that can emotionally recharge you as a couple—a trip to the mountains, a series of counseling sessions or sharing a hobby—helps prevent one or both of you from collapsing under the strain, leaving important things unsaid, or becoming bitter.

The Custody Trial Revisited

When you enter a custody case for the second time, you may think of yourself as an old pro who can take anything your ex-spouse, the lawyers and the judicial system can dish out. After all, you've been through it all before. So it may surprise you when you reenter the cycle and experience the same painful feelings of shock, anger, powerlessness and depression.

The shock reaction now involves you "waking up" and finding yourself in the middle of a new custody case. You suddenly ask yourself, "What on earth am I doing?" You doubt your sanity at the thought of subjecting yourself to all this again. This is the beginning of the self-doubt that pervades Custody Trial II. You've committed in external ways to the custody battle. The retainer has been paid, the legal paperwork signed, the initial court counselor appointment has been set. Things may seem to be moving too fast, after months, or more probably, years of waiting.

In addition, when you return to court for the second or third time, you've likely lost that naive trust you once had that good will triumph. Ideally, at this point you have been practicing for some time letting go of things you cannot control. But now you may see the reality of the court case with almost too much clarity and at times wish to return to the haze of blind faith you had the first time around. You consciously await the endless personal questionings and insulting insinuations that punctuate custody cases. You now don't bother to fantasize that the judge will see what a good person and loving parent you are. You realize how very much is out of your hands. As attorney Louis Kiefer writes in *How to Win Custody*,

> More often than not, a custody case will be decided neither on the facts of the case nor on the law of the land but on the secret and not-so-secret predilections and prejudices of attorneys, family relations officers and judges who are involved in the case. Very often none of these persons are schooled, trained or experienced in the subject of custody. They will have no uniform attitude

toward the subject but instead will depend on their own private experiences and attitudes.

Once again, it seems you've put your fate and happiness into the hands of a bunch of strangers. At times, you may be tempted to simply quit. You may even go so far as to tell the attorney to forget the whole thing in an attempt to cut your losses before the situation worsens. You need extra emotional support at this time, whether from a lawyer, your new spouse, a self-help group, a counselor, or a friend. Feeling discouraged in the midst of a custody case doesn't necessarily indicate an unfavorable outcome. Dramatic mood swings between the elation of thinking "I will get my child back" one moment and the self-deprecation of "I'm such a fool to even think about getting custody" the next moment, characterize the parent who goes back to court.

The anger of Custody Trial II can unfortunately be as unmitigated as that of Custody Trial I. The stress of your case, fraught with uncertainties and demands, builds up unexpectedly. Suddenly, you may find yourself flying into a rage in situations you were normally able to handle in the past. It is hoped that by now you are more aware of your anger and are more at ease with talking assertively to the instigator of your anger. Even if you're afraid to tell your attorney you're upset with him or her, try releasing your frustrations by talking about them with a friend, counselor or your new spouse. Deliberately let go of your anger in nondestructive ways (chapter 3) to avoid "burning your bridges."

The philosophy of the Serenity Prayer (chapter 4) can help you with anger, too. Use the power of your anger to address the things that you *can* influence—namely, what is said in court about you in praise of your good qualities. Let your anger energize those efforts.

Perhaps the most difficult part of the second custody trial is the depression. Anxiety, self-doubt, and disappointment are par for the course as the case goes on. The new custody case will probably go on for some months. Court dates are postponed and investigations yield ambiguous results. Your ex-spouse asks for a continuance on a case you thought was coming to a close. Your boss's patience wears thin as you ask for days off work to appear in court. Sleeplessness, a woe-is-me listlessness and susceptibility to illness all tend to plague parents at this stage. Suicidal thoughts are not uncommon. The stresses you face in a court situation are oftentimes extraordinary stresses. Until the case is settled, and the terrible pressure is removed, pursuing your now established good-mental-health routine may not be enough. This creates a scary dilemma for some parents: namely, if you get psychological counseling, will your ex-spouse find out about it and use it against you?

On the one hand, I strongly believe that anyone suffering from stress-related symptoms such as crying spells, hallucinations, sleep or appetite changes, mood swings, psychosomatic illness or pain, and especially thoughts of death or suicide, should seek professional mental health assistance. On the other hand, you may be asked the following question during your court appearance—I was: "Have you ever been seen by a counselor or psychologist?"

The possibility does exist that one or both opposing ex-spouses will try to use one another's history of psychological counseling as a weapon. If it is known that one parent has had counseling, it is possible that his or her counselor could be subpoenaed. However, many, many people of all different walks of life seek therapy of various kinds these days, and it no longer carries the stigma it once did. It is quite possible to prove that you are a better, healthier parent because you have received such help, and judges, investigators, social workers, and mediators routinely recommend counseling to troubled families. If you go for help related to alcohol or drug addiction, you should know that many rulings go against chemically dependent parents on the grounds that a relapse is too likely to occur. But judges in many instances have ruled that a completely sober parent is better than one who still drinks socially. A great deal depends on the length of time you've been clean and sober and your apparent ongoing commitment to your sobriety. There are no easy answers to this question. Remember, though, that there is no general record kept anywhere which lists people who receive mental health treatment. If you don't volunteer the fact that you have been going to therapy sessions to anyone—including your children and other relatives and friends who may not be discreet—then no one will find out without your consent.

If you find yourself suffering under the weight of the uncertainty of your case, get help early on. Probably one of the worst fears of parents in this situation is that they will buckle under the pressure while appearing in court. A sad case in point was that of my client, Henry.

His second custody battle had been a nightmare for Henry, thirty-five. He wanted his seven-year-old daughter, Cathy, to live with him. Henry's ex-wife, Robin, was counter-suing, alleging that Henry had been physically abusive to Cathy and had slapped her in the face on numerous occasions. These allegations, which Henry claimed were completely untrue, resulted in an intense investigation. Henry's home was inspected and he underwent many hours of questioning by social workers. He said, "I knew I needed help because I had no one to turn to. But I was so afraid that if I saw a psychologist, someone from the court would find out, and then my wife would *really* have a field day with me and smear my name around royally!" Henry became determined to "handle this thing on my own." But he did nothing to actually handle it; he just let his hurt and resentment build up inside.

One day, after eight months of investigations, Henry and Robin had to appear together in a court-appointed social worker's office:

> Robin was telling this lady how I used to whip Cathy with a belt, and I was sitting there biting my lip and trying not to get too upset. Then she started talking about how I had abused *her*, too! That was it. I just lost it right then and there and I started screaming. I'd never lost control like that, ever. I was just so stressed out and mad at Robin. From then on, it was downhill, because that social worker began to believe Robin. I really made myself look bad.

Henry wept as he told this story. In the end, his visitation periods with Cathy were reduced and a third person was required to be present at all times.

The lesson learned from what happened to Henry is: while you cannot prevent stress from occurring when it comes from external sources, remember that you *do* have control over when and how you will react to that stress. For many people, a second custody suit is more stressful than the first. There seems to be even more at stake. It feels like the last chance. But the last chance for what? The last chance for happiness? By now I hope you know this isn't true. The last chance to be close to your child? You know that this, too, isn't true.

However, it may indeed be the last practical chance to have your child living with you full-time. This is the reality you have to accept before entering into another custody suit.

Transcending Custodial Status

The life of a parent without primary custody can seem to be defined by a temporary void, in limbo between losing custody and gaining it back. You're chronically waiting for something, waiting for that moment when you'll make contact with your children again.

If you truly do not want custody, yet try for it anyway, you're putting your children, yourself, and your family through needless anguish. You may be avoiding facing your own feelings of guilt, low self-worth and inadequacy: what kind of person, you wonder, doesn't want custody of his or her own kids? On the other hand, if you desire custody and continue to avoid returning to court, you feel you are missing out on that chance to feel better about yourself because you at least tried, even if the chances are slim. If you're still undecided, it's up to you to look at why you haven't come to a resolution. Are you afraid of getting custody? Are you afraid of being the "loser" again? Could you handle not getting custody after the enormous emotional and financial investment? If you're not ready to decide, why can't you put the draining "should I/shouldn't I's" behind you until you are ready?

Only you can unravel these thorny issues for yourself. Neither this book nor anyone around you can do your griefwork for you, speed up the process, or make the decision for you in a way that will leave you satisfied with yourself.

The important point is: *don't* put your relationship with your children on hold, no matter how negative you feel about your custody status. The special bond between you and your children should be cared for and nurtured for the precious treasure it is, not because of legal ramifications or future plans.

11
Women without Custody and Men without Custody: Some Special Considerations

Nothing feels quite right until I have my visits with my little boy. Until then, I just don't feel complete. Like a part of me is missing or something.

> —Twenty-three-year-old mother
> without custody, one year after
> her ex-husband won custody of
> their three-year-old son

The year was 1978. The movie *Kramer vs. Kramer* shocked audiences across the United States, proving to be both a boon and a hindrance to divorcing parents. Joanna Kramer was portrayed as a vulnerable character—emotionally overwrought and pushed to the edge. Yet, when she walked out the door abandoning her husband, Ted, and small son, audiences were unforgiving. When, in visible torment, she eventually relinquished permanent custody of their son to Ted, audiences clapped and cheered. They felt she didn't deserve to have custody. The boy, audiences felt, clearly belonged with his father.

Although the portrait the film painted of the noncustodial woman certainly didn't enhance her status, it did at least bring her out of hiding. And suddenly, it became common knowledge that fathers want and will fight hard for custody.

Women without Custody: Looking at the Stereotype

Before *Kramer vs. Kramer* and before the advent of support groups like Mothers Without Custody, the woman who lost custody of her children was often left to wonder secretly, "Am I the only mother in the world who is apart from her children?"

Actually, she is one among two and a half million mothers without custody, whose ranks continue to swell as more and more fathers ask for and win custody of their kids. The numbers will also continue to grow as mothers voluntarily surrender custody to their ex-husbands, usually because of financial stresses. In addition, a growing population of women are admitting that they simply don't feel they're cut out for motherhood and that their husbands are better parents. This option has become more acceptable in just the last few years.

The plight of the noncustodial mother is often lonely. She's frequently unwilling to talk about her story, choosing instead to feel guilty and miserable within herself. She may be painfully aware of society's negative image of mothers without custody because she believes in the stereotype herself. But now, she senses, these stigmas are applied to *her*. Now she's the one others wonder about. She feels self-conscious about the questions others are asking about her behind her back. Was she an unfit mother? Did she abuse or neglect her kids? Abandon them? Maybe she's an alcoholic or had an affair. How in the world could she lose custody of her kids, anyway?

My friend Crystal tells this story of hiding her noncustodial status. She had been without custody for six months when she met Jon. She didn't tell him about her children, for fear of "turning him off." She says, "It was so nervewracking, hiding the fact that I had kids from Jon! I had to hide my pictures of them, and when they'd come to visit, I'd have to make excuses for not being able to be with him."

Four months into her relationship with Jon, Crystal and her children went to the beach. As Crystal and her children walked hand-in-hand along the beach, she felt relaxed and at ease. Then she heard a voice.

"Crystal! Is that *you*?" It was Jon, and the first thing he wanted to know was who the kids belonged to. She stammered some explanation, but the more she talked, the redder Jon's face grew. It was the last time she saw him.

On those occasions when a mother without custody risks sharing the secret of her noncustodial status with others, she defensively blurts out answers to questions that haven't even been asked. "Yes, of course I love my kids." "Yes I want them desperately." "I lost them because of my attorney who. . . ." "My ex-husband told vicious lies about me in court."

"No one understands how or why I lost custody," exclaimed Viola, still determined to make someone understand how she felt. "When people find out they usually say, 'Vi, there's nothing wrong with you, so why did you lose your kids?' The answer always sticks in my throat, because they're implying that only women who have something wrong with them lose custody. But it's not that simple at all! So, I just usually end up either giving them a real short explanation or else I embarrass myself by going into too much detail. On the one hand, I want them to know that I'm not a bad person. That I didn't lose custody on account of abusing my kids or anything like that. But I also feel like it's really none of their business, either." Viola raised her palms and shoulders in a "What's a person to do?" pose and tried to laugh. She caught a tear before it could roll down her cheek.

Many a mother without custody eventually vows never to tell another soul about her custodial status. In fact, she often won't even reveal she has kids. All the while, she dreads the seemingly innocent question—frequently an icebreaker among women—"Do you have children?"

If you are not a mother without custody, at this point you may be asking yourself, "What's the big deal? Why is she trying to hide it?"

The answer to this question could probably fill several volumes. Certainly, it's partly the residue of the old "maternal presumption" practice. There was a time in the not-too-distant past, and this seems to stick firmly in the minds of people with no knowledge of current custody procedures, when the mother was automatically awarded custody unless she was destitute, insane, alcoholic, or morally reprehensible. If she was any of these things, the children were taken away from her for their welfare. And the stereotype of a woman who voluntarily surrenders custody goes something like this: she is a cold, selfish woman who unthinkingly brought children into this world, got tired of them, and abandoned them.

Both this stereotyping of women who are apart from their kids and the "maternal presumption" practice are outgrowths of a biocultural bias we all share—our reverence of Mother with a capital "M," what Jung identifed as one of, if not the most, universal of all cultural archetypes. Obviously, this is because women are biologically destined to bear the next generation. Not quite as obvious now as it once was, but certainly still taken for granted, is that it is also her destiny, her obligation, her privilege, to raise and nurture the next generation. It's lodged in the deepest part of our cultural consciousness, and, even as "consciousness-raising" continues to take place, many women do consider this their most important job.

Feminist scholars Laurel Richardson and Verta Taylor in their book, *Feminist Frontiers*, point out, however, that

> . . . social, biological and psychological sciences often nonconsciously borrow the ideological presumptions of their culture and repackage them as scientific truths and facts. So, for example, the assumption that women *should* want to be mothers becomes the basis for psychological and sociological theories of motherhood. . . . Women who choose not to mother are viewed as deviants, social problems, and immature.

It seems this bias can be and is applied to women who, although they have borne children rightly enough, choose to or are forced by circumstances to live without their children.

The mother without custody receives the unmistakable message that there is something fundamentally *wrong* with her on several levels. She isn't doing what's most important for her to do (that is, mother her child), so probably her values are badly confused or she is as yet emotionally undeveloped. Or, if it's not her "fault" that she lost her kids, she is still less of a woman for it. This is the inevitable conclusion when we narrowly define woman as "person who mothers."

When faced with this negative attitude, the primary self-affirmation for you, a mother without custody, should be: "Even though my kids aren't physically with me all the time, I am still, in the most critical ways, their mother. I, in fact, have not stopped mothering." Enumerate for yourself what the critical aspects of motherhood are—in effect, write the story of your love for your child. How it was in the beginning, how it changed form, and yet stayed the same. You can even write this as a long letter addressed to your child.

For those women who still tend to see themselves as incomplete or unnatural because they don't live with their kids, it may help to look at the concept of motherhood in terms of recent history. In *Women and Self-Esteem*, authors Linda Tschirhart Sanford and Mary Ellen Donovan find that "there have been large shifts in the extent to which [motherhood] has been revered and emphasized'':

> It wasn't until the end of World War II that a full-blown mystique developed around motherhood. . . . During the war women proved they could keep the country going as well as men could, and they could do any jobs men could do. . . . But once the war was over, men wanted their jobs back, and so women were forced out of their wartime posts. To facilitate the process . . . the U.S. government mounted a huge propaganda campaign whose message, in a nutshell, was that a woman's proper place was in the maternity ward having babies or at home taking care of them.

Women in this country, especially those who came of age in the fifties and sixties, have good cause to question their deepest beliefs about what it means to be a good mother and where these beliefs came from. What is your definition of "mother"? How does, in your personal belief system, an ideal mother behave? Why is this the ideal situation? In what ways have you deviated from this ideal and how do you feel about it? Can you and should you revise your definition of what it means to be a good mother?

Ruth was fingering a well-defined wrinkle extending from her nose to her mouth. The fifty-eight-year-old woman had come to a day-long self-help seminar. She patiently listened to a woman in her group describe her divorce. Then it was Ruth's turn.

"Well," she began reluctantly, "I was divorced in 1958." She coughed and the others looked at her impatiently as if to say, "Get to the point, lady!" Ruth's eyes reddened and she unsnapped her purse to get a tissue. The group's counselor took Ruth's hand and reassured her that it was okay to talk.

"It was nearly thirty years ago when my husband took my five kids away from me after our divorce," she choked out tearfully. She stopped and blew her nose into the tightly wrung tissue.

"What are your feelings about the loss, Ruth?" the counselor asked gently.

"Well, I, uh, I'm sad of course!" she snapped.

"You seem to be quite angry about it," the counselor replied.

"No, I'm not angry at all! I'm sad, I told you! Now why don't you listen to me!"

"You're not angry with your ex-husband for taking your kids?"

"No! Damn it, no! I keep telling you, I'm not angry!"

Although Ruth was unaware of it, bitter anger came through her every spoken word. Ruth explained that religious beliefs prohibited her from expressing anger and maybe she couldn't feel her anger. But everyone around her certainly could.

The negative feelings we have about ourselves and the system following custody loss don't go away just by virtue of growing older. Ruth and others like her who lost custody many years ago were more unfortunate in many ways than mothers without custody today. As recently as ten years ago, the idea that women lost or gave up custody was practically unheard of and rarely discussed publicly. The woman who lost custody in years past often had no one to turn to for support or comfort. Recovery from the custody crisis would certainly be hastened by the elimination of the prejudice surrounding noncustodial women, but the task of feeling better about her lot in life is still primarily the responsibility of the woman herself. If she waits for attitudes to change, she may be like Ruth—bitter and out of touch with her feelings many years after her custody loss. So, as a noncustodial woman facing other people's prejudiced attitudes, realize that you really cannot afford to judge yourself by other people's standards of womanhood.

Of course, being aware of prejudice and knowing where it comes from doesn't always make it easier to deal with. But we are living in a time when women devoting their lives exclusively to their kids is more ideology than reality. "Only 6 percent of all Americans still live in families with a working father, a homemaker mother, and dependent children," a recent article in *Ms.* magazine announces. Not having children at all has become a respectable alternative for women.

It is no longer necessary to buy the stereotype. For our own future and our children's future, it is necessary for us to like and accept ourselves, no matter what our custodial status.

Reaching Out

My own recovery from the stigma of being a noncustodial mother was long in coming. I struggled with low self-esteem because part of me believed that something had to be very wrong with me because I didn't have my kids. While it seemed all the other mommies in the world were shopping with a kid in their grocery cart, my cart sat empty. While all the other mothers got hugs and construction paper flowers on Mother's Day, I was lucky if I got a phone call from my children. I felt sad, different, and very alone.

It certainly didn't help that I kept my custody status a secret. During my three years in the "custody closet," I was absolutely certain that if people knew my horrible secret they would reject me. And since I was essentially living a lie in not allowing anyone to really know me, I felt unloved. I was bitter and full of regrets. Every day I'd think, "If only I hadn't sent the boys back to their father that night. If only. . . ."

My healing came only after I shed this negative conception of myself. After I started working as a counselor, my first noncustodial client was a man who desperately missed his children. He was a good person and he was in pain. He didn't, I realized, lose his integrity when he lost custody of his children. Although I never revealed my own custody loss to him, I knew that I hurt just a little bit less because of helping him through his custody crisis.

My work with that noncustodial father opened new doors for me. From then on, it seemed that I was seeing more and more clients who were without custody of their children. Their pain was deep and very familiar to me. But suddenly my own loss didn't seem so meaningless anymore. Suddenly, peace of mind was a possibility. I still didn't like the fact that I was without my sons, but I no longer let it rob me of the happiness life had to offer.

By helping others, I was able to make some sense out of a situation which, to me, was otherwise cruelly senseless. Joining a support group, sharing with and helping others, can in the same way be the vital element in turning your custody crisis around and starting down the long road to acceptance.

Mothers Without Custody is a national, nonprofit support group for noncustodial mothers. Many large cities hold regular meetings. This organization was founded by Ellen Kimball, an insurance claims adjuster who voluntarily surrendered custody of her two children to her ex-husband in 1980. She made the decision because medical problems kept her sedated and bedridden for an extended period of time. Her ex-husband agreed to take the children, but only on a permanent basis. Kimball and the children's father worked out a mutually satisfactory agreement through which she would pay child support and have generous visitation privileges.

But Kimball wasn't ready for the overwhelming criticism she was to receive. The reactions of others consistently smacked of shock and outrage that she would "give her children away." Not one to crumble over the opinions of others, Kimball began meeting with other noncustodial women to discuss the unjust stigmas, the powerful feelings surrounding custody loss and ways to deal with these problems.

This original Boston group of Mothers Without Custody became the springboard for the national organization. Membership is now open to noncustodial or previously noncustodial mothers as well as to women in joint-custodial arrangements.

Among its objectives are:

—To enhance the quality of life for member's children by strengthening the role of noncustodial parents in regard to custody, child support, visitation and parenting.

—To provide a support network and outlet for sharing experiences among mothers without physical custody of their children.

—To educate and inform the public in order to dispel biases against the single-parent child and the single-parent household.

—Finally, to serve as a liaison between members and those organizations and individuals whose special interest is the child's well-being, health, and happiness. (Information about how to contact this organization appears at the end of the book.)

Support groups provide a safe forum to talk about your tears and joys. Others accept your feelings as important and legitimate and you, in turn, accept them also. When you're surrounded by people who affirm your worth, you reconsider other people's negative views of you. You realize that you must embark on your own lifelong process of self-definition. Through this process, you find yourself on the other, more comforting side of the custody crisis, a place full of knowing "who I am," of growth and, most importantly, self-love.

Men without Custody: Looking at the Stereotype

Mothers without custody are today able to openly refuse to accept the past ways they were categorized, and by the way they live their lives, serve as an example to other women who may need to do the same rethinking. The noncustodial man who openly admits to missing his children is also in a way the modern rebel. Being a man without custody means having a chance to reassess what it means to be a successful, fulfilled man and a good father.

This "New Man" listens to his own feelings instead of succumbing to the attitude that a divorced man's lot in life is to unemotionally and calmly accept custody loss. He refutes the notion that the children's needs can best be met by their mother. He is as willing as a woman counterpart to take time off work and skip overtime and after-work socializing for the sake of his kids.

He is justifiably angry when he encounters suspicion as to his motives and when others assume, "He just wants to get out of paying child support." He is made defensive as others patronize him, saying in various ways, "There, there, of course you want your children." The myth is that, as a newly divorced man, he's in bed with a different woman every night. The truth is that newly divorced fathers without custody go home to empty, lonely houses just as their counterparts do.

The paradox is that we stamp "acceptable" on men who surrender custody while practically pinning a scarlet letter on women who do so. And while women without custody are supposed to have strong, anguished emotional reactions to losing custody, men are somehow supposed to take it in stride. The differences continue in that while many women keep their noncustodial status a secret, men are more open about their custody status, even joking (although how funny it is remains a separate question) about who among their friends pays the most child support and alimony. But when women do admit to a trusted confidant that their kids don't live with them anymore, they usually are able to express their hurt and grief freely. Men more commonly guard their feelings concerning custody loss and hide the fact that they're emotionally wounded.

Men and women feel equally guilty for a family break-up. But in the man's case, saying "I'm responsible" may follow the socially imposed edict that the man is the provider for and protector of the family. Any harm that came to the family happened because he didn't ward it off. The Father, in Jungian terminology, provides "structure." The Mother's duty is to nurture. Obviously, the problem is that we think of these roles—Nurturer and Structure-giver—as being determined by gender. Examining the same faulty logic, Geoffrey Grief notes in *Single Fathers* that

> When a father has custody, people assume he is an extraordinary man. They think he must be incredibly dedicated to his children.

. . . At the same time, dichotomously, he is seen as someone who needs help. How can he know how to cook, clean and shop for clothes with his children? How can he know how to discuss sexuality with an adolescent daughter? People feel sorry for him and run to his aid. They feel sorry for his children.

Fathers, goes the stereotype, are not natural nurturers; some woman has got to be around to put band-aids on the kids' knees.

Of course, children need both structure and nurturance. Which parent provides which is irrelevant and one parent can provide both. The depth and quality of love and the desire to comfort, cherish, and teach can be equal for both male and female parents. For it is finally acceptable for men to abandon the old macho "pillar of strength" father ideal. Geoffrey Grief notes that, since the 1950s,

. . . many men have thought about their own childhood and concluded they missed something when they were growing up because their father either was not home as a result of a demanding work schedule, or was distant when he was at home. Fathers want to give their children a different experience, and they want a different parenting experience for themselves than their own fathers had.

Noncustodial fathers benefit from this blurring of traditional ideas of what fathers are and what fathers do. If you are a man without custody, your emotional pain at being apart from your children doesn't need further justification or explanation, any more than a woman's pain of the same kind. So, when you run up against the prejudice that you don't need or miss your children as much as a woman would, your self-affirmation should be, "I love my children deeply and need to have them near me. My demonstrations of my love for them and joy in being with them are a big part of what makes me a good father."

Since you can be a sensitive and loving person without forsaking a strong sense of masculinity, realize now that you cannot afford the high price of lost closeness with your children that comes with living by other people's definitions of masculinity.

As the divorce rate continues to be very high, there will be more and more single fathers, and the fact that men make high quality nurturers will become more accepted. In turn, more and more men will sue for custody.

However, it will probably be many years before men stand an equal chance of receiving custody. While a recent study by psychologist Phyllis Chesler indicated that fathers who fight for custody have up to a seventy percent chance of receiving it, the U.S. Census Bureau reports that national averages for divorcing men who get custody remain at about ten percent among all divorces. The difference between these two statistics is probably due to the fact that still few men actually ask for custody. But the numbers are rapidly growing.

What does the trend toward more men asking for and receiving custody mean to the man who already went to court and lost custody because he didn't ask for it? He's angry and guilty. When Dennis went through a divorce five years ago, it didn't occur to him to ask for custody. "My lawyer knew my feelings about the kids," he says. "He knew that I was worried how they'd do with Debbie being the only parent in the home, but he didn't even suggest that I try to get custody!" A father in this position also fears his children will think he must not love them very much.

If this describes your current situation, there are several things you can do. You should make it your highest priority to communicate your love for your children notwithstanding the custody arrangements. Also give some thought to family counseling for you and your children, even if it's been some time since the divorce. This is an excellent opportunity to bring out and deal with harbored resentments. (It also means facing the fear that your children cannot handle the fact that you're not perfect.) Review and answer very carefully the questions that are raised in chapter 10. Would it be in your children's best interests for you to sue for custody now? This is the critical question, no matter how bad you feel about missed opportunities in the past. If it would not be best thing for your children, give yourself permission to let go of the guilt.

One final consideration in light of all these new trends is the dad who honestly feels incompetent or unqualified to be a full-time parent, or who strongly believes that, individual parenting skills aside, children belong with their mother. There is a strong probability that in the future these men will feel the pressure to jump on the bandwagon and initiate custody battles. If this happens, the traditional man may wrestle, just as women have, with terrible guilt as he faces the fact that "I really don't want custody."

Support Groups for Men

Somehow, the hard times don't seem as though they were completely in vain when we can share the knowledge gained from them. By joining forces, noncustodial fathers support one another emotionally and work toward reforming unfair aspects of child custody laws. There are several national support groups for noncustodial men. Among the largest and best known is Fathers of America.

Fathers of America helps noncustodial fathers form and maintain local support groups. Most meetings feature guest speakers who have expertise concerning divorce and child custody. The group's purpose is to "support the idea that children need both parents after divorce, as well as before." In addition, it seeks to "help parents make a realistic assessment of their situation and show them the steps to take to maximize their chances of securing joint custody of their children."

Support groups work. Participation in one allows you to share your story with others who truly understand, make close friendships, and become a good listener. If there is no support group in your area, contact a national group for information on how to start up your own group. You'll have no trouble finding others who share your situation.

Both mothers and fathers have the opportunity to make things better for one another. Consider that most people are not judging you personally when they express negative or patronizing views of your custody status. Many people are afraid *not* to judge. They feel they are expected to be stunned by your situation. They are following the societal script but probably have done very little serious thinking about the subject. I firmly believe that noncustodial parents can teach the public how to treat them. Think for a moment about what you can do to educate another about parents without custody. Can you write an article for your local paper or work/community/club newsletter? Give a speech at a civic club or another club you belong to? Start a support group? Without a doubt, when someone says something hurtful in regard to your relationship with your kids, you can compassionately set him or her straight. Whatever you can do, do it. All parents without custody will benefit.

*   *   *

Rebuilding

After an earthquake levels a building, you rebuild, starting by making the foundation as strong as it can be. You add pieces bit by bit, and only after you've done quite a bit of groundwork can you see how other pieces fit in. The process is slow and painstaking, as you recognize past flaws and innovate ways not to repeat them—you are trying to build something that will stand for a long, long time. Probably, you would have preferred not to have to rebuild at all, but you've got to—you've got to expend the effort or you'll have nothing but the remains of the old building. In the end, your new building is stronger than the one that stood before.

Your relationship with your kids now is not the same one you had before. Your life is not the same as it was before. It is natural for you to regret this, to wish with all your might that you could have the old way back.

But do not only wish for the old way. This leaves your life fragmented—with rubble (bad memories and past, negative behaviors); some scattered, but useful building blocks (good memories and positive skills); and a basic foundation (your love for your child). But there's no wholeness to work toward.

Envision a new way. Begin your new structure. Let go of the bad and make renewed use of the good. Your life and your connection with your child will be different. And they will be stronger and better.

In closing I'd like to remind you of another saying that comes to us from the tradition of Alcoholics Anonymous: Progress, not perfection.

The process of working toward that stronger, better, whole structure—setbacks included—is the important thing. As long as you are a builder in life, in parenting, in love relationships, in friendships, you will enjoy the byproduct we call happiness.

Wherever you are in your journey as a parent and a person, may happiness be yours.

Epilogue

I had been a noncustodial mother for about two years when the idea of writing *My Kids Don't Live with Me Anymore* first entered my mind. I'd envisioned a way to help others deal with some of the pain I'd endured, but what I didn't foresee was the powerful effect this book would have on my own life.

Writing about my custody crisis meant that I first had to reexperience some extremely painful memories. As I wrote about depression, I again felt the anguish of missing my boys. When describing anger, I *was* furious with myself and a legal system that I felt had let me down. Each day when I sat down at the typewriter, I knew that my emotions would lead me onto the roller coaster of the custody crisis one more time. But that process, though painful, was also healing some wounds that I hadn't known still existed. I started thinking more and more about the possibility of regaining custody.

I first approached a lawyer about a second custody battle as I was completing the first draft of the manuscript. Writing the book, it turned out, was removing some of the emotional blocks that had kept me from feeling brave enough to withstand fighting for custody—and possibly losing it—a second time.

By the time the first draft was complete, I felt renewed, strong, and certain that I wanted my children to live with me again. I closely examined *why* I wanted this, and I talked about it at length with my sons, husband, parents, friends and lawyer. I got a lot of encouraging, but cautious, support. I knew the odds were against me—courts rarely decide to change custody unless very strong reasons for doing so can be proven—but I felt my reasons were healthy and I had to try.

So, while I was revising the first draft of this book, I entered into my second custody suit. And, I actually went through a second round of grief stages while I was writing about them. The too-familiar feelings of guilt, frustration, anger, and unbearable depression lived with me while I was describing them on paper. Life was truly imitating art!

My second custody case was an almost indescribably painful experience. It lasted nearly two years, and some of the legal aspects aren't completely settled today. I risked being fired for taking so much time off work and spent thousands of dollars in legal fees. But the worst part was the torture of continually wondering how it would all turn out. Second-round custody cases often backfire, and I was afraid the whole thing would blow up in my face at any moment. Instead of receiving custody, I could have received reduced visitation rights and an order to pay increased child support.

One time, I was ready to call the whole thing off. I was convinced that I was going to lose, and it seemed futile to be putting my children, my second husband and myself through so much pain. At that point everyone I talked to agreed that withdrawing from the suit would be best. But luckily I consulted one more person before making the call to my lawyer. My dear friend Melinda took me by the shoulders and gently shook me. "You CAN'T give up, Doreen," she told me firmly while piercing me with a dead-still stare. "You must fight for those children!" Thank God I listened to her.

The irony of all this is that now, as I complete the final draft of *My Kids Don't Live with Me Anymore*, I can announce to you that I was awarded custody. Chuck and Grant have been living with me since December 1986.

I have now seen the custody crisis from both sides of the fence—as a noncustodial parent and as a custodial parent. I started this book by saying that the custody crisis—the pain, the fear, and the intermittent joy—never ends; it simply changes form. I now more than ever feel and know the truth of my own words.

I cannot pretend that I'm not overjoyed to have custody. Of course I am. But the moment when I began to really live again was not the moment when I was awarded custody. No, the true turning point came when I began to believe in myself and forgive myself. Then I found the courage to learn how to begin rebuilding. And that's when I knew my sons and I were going to be all right.

Support Groups

A letter or telephone call is all that's needed to gain information about local chapters of the following support groups for parents.

Fathers of America
P.O. Box 3075
Santa Monica, CA 90403

Mothers Without Custody
P.O. Box 56762
Houston, TX 77256-6762

Parents Without Partners International Office
8807 Colesville Road
Silver Springs, MD 20910   (301) 588-9394

Stepfamily Association of America
602 East Joppa Road
Towson, MD 21204   (301) 823-7570

Bibliography

Bienenfeld, Florence, Ph.D. *Helping Your Child Succeed After Divorce*. Claremont, California: Hunter House, Inc., Publishers, 1987.

Bozarth-Campbell, Alla, Ph.D. *Life Is Goodbye/Life Is Hello*. Minneapolis: CompCare Publishers, 1982.

Frankl, Viktor E. *Man's Search for Meaning*. New York: Pocket Books, 1984.

Grief, Geoffrey. *Single Fathers*. Lexington, Massachusetts: Lexington Books, 1985.

Hootman, Marcia and Patt Perkins. *How to Forgive Your Ex-Husband and Get on with Your Life*. New York: Warner Books, Inc., 1985.

Kiefer, Louis. *How to Win Custody*. New York: Simon & Schuster, 1982.

Keleman, Stanley. *Living Your Dying*. New York: Random House, Inc., 1974.

Kopp, Sheldon. *If You Meet the Buddha on the Road, Kill Him!* New York: Bantam Books, 1976.

Kubler-Ross, Elisabeth, M.D. *On Death and Dying*. New York: MacMillan Publishing Co., 1969.

May, Rollo. *Psychology and the Human Dilemma*. New York: W.W. Norton & Co., 1980.

Naifeh, Steven and Gregory White Smith. *Why Can't Men Open Up?* New York: Clarkson N. Potter, Inc., 1984.

Paul, Jordan, Ph.D. and Margaret Paul, Ph.D. *If You Really Loved Me*. Minneapolis: CompCare Publishers, 1987.

Richardson, Laurel and Verta Taylor. *Feminist Frontiers: Rethinking Sex, Gender, and Society*. Reading, Massachusetts: Addison-Wesley Publishing Co., 1983.

Sanford, Linda Tschirhart and Mary Ellen Donovan. *Women and Self-Esteem*. New York: Penguin Books, 1984.

Spiegel, Yorick. *The Grief Process*. Nashville: Abingdon, 1977.

Viorst, Judith. *Necessary Losses*. New York: Ballantine Books, 1987.

Suggested Reading

In addition to the books listed in the bibliography, the following books may prove useful in your personal healing process:

The Cinderella Complex by Colette Dowling (Simon and Schuster, 1981). For anyone who has ever felt "I can't do it on my own," Ms. Dowling has written a book for overcoming this fear of independence. Especially useful for newly-divorced persons who are trying to adjust to living alone and being completely responsible for themselves.

A Day at a Time (CompCare Publishers, 1976). Although this little book was written primarily for people struggling with addictions, it would be valuable to anyone. Each page has an inspirational writing—one for every day of the year. The text for each day is short and quick-reading for those who are in a hurry in the morning, but it lends itself equally as well to those who have time to meditate. Either way, it offers a "pick-me-up" to help one feel good throughout the day.

Games Divorced People Play by Dr. Melvyn A. Berk and Joanne B. Grant (Prentice-Hall, 1981). This book outlines some of the common psychological and emotional "traps" that divorced people can fall into. These patterns keep divorced people from attaining their post-divorce goals. Ways to recognize, avoid, and undo these traps are described.

The Hazards of Being Male: Surviving the Myth of Masculine Privilege by Herb Goldberg, Ph.D. (Signet, 1976). Fathers who are struggling with the myth that men shouldn't feel or show their grief will find this book very comforting. It explains where many myths about masculinity came from and how to overcome or learn to live with them.

The New Assertive Woman by Lynn Z. Bloom, Karen Coburn, and Joan Perlman (Dell Publishing Co., 1975). Recommended for both men and women. Learning assertiveness is a vital part of stress management. Readers will find themselves feeling stronger and stronger with each page!

Positive Imaging by Norman Vincent Peale (Ballantine Books, 1982). This inspirational book may be just the medicine needed to lift the spirits of parents enduring the custody crisis. Although it has religious overtones, it is not "preachy." It offers uplifting hope in a quick-reading text.

Stress Breakers by Helene Lerner with Roberta Elins (CompCare Publishers, 1986). This fun, fast-paced book offers many valuable tips and insights about surviving the various stresses in our everyday lives. Especially useful for those who don't feel they have a lot of time to read about stress management; each stress breaker is based on a proven method for reducing tension and anxiety.

Sweet Suffering: Women as Victims by Natalie Shainess, M.D. (Simon and Schuster, 1984). Although this book was written primarily for women, its message would apply equally well to any man who has ever felt 1) that the world is picking on him, or 2) that he's constantly putting his foot in his mouth. This excellent book provides "survival instruction"—the nuts and bolts of how to stop sabotaging your own success.

Why Am I Afraid to Tell You Who I Am? by John Powell (Argus Communications, 1969). This now-classic book helps those who have difficulty expressing feelings to others. A must for parents who are in the "custody closet," or who feel all alone in their grief.

Books about children and parenting:

The Custody Handbook by Persia Wooley (Summit Books, 1979).

Father Power by Henry Biller and Dennis Meredith (David McKay, 1974).

How to Win as a Stepfamily by Emily and John Vishner (Dembner Books, 1982).

Mom's House, Dad's House by Isolina Ricci (MacMillan, 1980).

Parents Book about Divorce by Richard A. Gardner (Doubleday and Co., 1977).

Perfect Parenting and Other Myths by Frank Main (CompCare Publishers, 1986).

Sharing Parenthood After Divorce: An Enlightened Child Custody Guide for Mothers, Fathers, and Kids by Ciji Ware (Viking Press, 1982).

Solo Parenting: Your Essential Guide by Kathleen McCoy (New American Library, 1987).

Surviving the Breakup by Judith S. Wallerstein and Joan Berlin Kelly (Basic Books, 1980).

Your Child's Self-Esteem by Dorothy Corkville Brings (Dolphin Books, 1975).

Books for children:

The Boys and Girls Book about Divorce by Richard A. Gardner (James Aronson, 1983).

The Boys and Girls Book about Stepfamilies by Richard A. Gardner (Creative Therapeutics, 1985).

The Divorce Workbook by Sally B. Ives (Waterfront Books, 1985).

How to Get It Together When Your Parents Are Coming Apart by Arlene Kramer Richards and Irene Willis (David McKay, 1976).

What's Going to Happen to Me?: When Parents Separate or Divorce by Eda J. Le Shan (MacMillan, 1986).